Our Honest Charlie Wood

Josephine Carr

MABEL PRESS

For Charlie's great grandchildren, Ian Wood and Sue Staines.

For my long suffering editor, Stephen Goldman.
In memory of Papa Aspin.

Charles Wood

First published 2019
Second Print

Cover artwork: Lis Lawrence
Cover design: Dominic Dyson
Copyright © 2019 Josephine Carr

A CIP catalogue record for this book is available from the British Library

ISBN: 978-1-9161301-0-4

Typeset in Clarendon and Baskerville
Printed and bound in Great Britain by
CPI Group (UK) Ltd, Croydon CR0 4YY

First published in Great Britain in 2019 by Mabel Press, Jevington

www.mabelpublishing.co.uk

The Author

Josephine Carr is a farmer and writer. She trained as a barrister before moving into journalism, editing and publishing several legal and financial magazines and directories, as well as writing columns for the Times and Evening Standard and regular articles for Eventing magazine. She also worked on a legal series for Channel 4.

She now runs a horse livery yard and sheep farm. Her grandfather, Fred Aspin, was a jump jockey in the 1920s. When he retired from riding he spent many years as the head groom at the stud in Jevington originally established by Charles Wood.

CONTENTS

Prologue

"A famous music hall act at the time, Fred Albert, used to improvise verses suited to the day's events. As he sang, magic lantern portraits of the celebrity would flash on the screen at the back of the hall.

'And now there comes before our eyes
A jockey true and good
Behold the prince of horsemen
Our honest Charlie Wood.'

Up would go a picture of Wood in a racing jacket, followed by applause and perhaps a few hisses from backers who had not been so lucky over Charlie."

The Gay Victorians, Ralph Nevill, 1930

The history of a time is written by the victor. That can prove awkward if the vanquished refuses to submit.

This is the story of a man the British racing establishment worked hard to destroy and then delete from the history books – with some success. The most well-known sportsman of his time has almost vanished from sight. His life and his achievements have been buried. His footnote in the history of the 1880s is as the "naughty boy" who shuffled off in disgrace: convenient but untrue.

Hidden behind that version of his life is the story of a boy from the slums of Hull who rose to challenge the aristocracy in a sport where, in the 19th century, they demanded complete submission. It is the story of the servant who rose to become a wealthy master in his own right, the supremely talented jockey who refused to go quietly when the Jockey Club banished him for nine years at the height of his career. It may be a story of a man who sailed close to the wind, but to accept the simple description of him as a rogue is to bow to the perpetrators of the injustice.

To the aristocracy who dominated racing in the 19th century he was known as Wood, or C Wood Up. To his family, friends and many admirers he was Charlie, Chas, Charley, or the Nation's Favourite Jockey – the three times winner of the Derby and all of the classic Blue Riband races.

Charles Wood rode for the highest in the land on the finest horses of the time. He gave few interviews, and the story of his life has not been told. In the histories of the time when he was pre-eminent, he appears mostly as a footnote. The authors refer to his successes only to emphasise how far he fell.

In the late 1800s the sport of kings was struggling to survive. Rumours of heavy betting, fixed races, horses nobbled and jockeys running betting rings threatened to engulf it. The Jockey Club, as the self-appointed regulator of racing, was losing control. It decided it needed to be seen to cleanse the Augean Stables and it set out to find a suitable scapegoat.

Once it had identified its target, it acted with a ruthlessness that made its own members uncomfortable and was condemned around the world.

CHAPTER ONE

Derby Day, 1897

Redemption

June 2nd 1897 dawns humid and misty over Epsom Downs. It is Derby Day, Queen Victoria's Diamond Jubilee Derby Day.

ARRIVALS.

"Arrival"
The Illustrated Sporting and Dramatic News, 1897
© Illustrated London News Ltd/Mary Evans

Charlie Wood has redemption in his sights as he walks out onto the famous course. He is filled with a determination to ride the race of his life. For most of the previous nine years the former champion jockey has not been allowed to set foot on any racecourse in the UK. Banished from every training ground. Forbidden even to ride a horse in a trial to test its ability and

4

forced to sue for libel. Warned off under Jockey Club rules used with a ferocity reserved just for him.

This is his moment. He is about to ride in the biggest sporting event of the year and the most famous race in the world. He will be seen and written about by the world's press, riding in front of the same members of the British aristocracy who had set out to ruin him 10 years earlier.

If he can win the Jubilee Derby in front of his enemies packed into the Jockey Club's uncomfortable stand by the finishing post, it will be a moment to savour. It will be impossible for them to deny his return to his rightful place as a leading jockey.

The rulers of racing want him to fail. They want him to go back into the shadows and this time stay there. They hope his age will deliver their wish. At 42 they think he is too old to succeed in the Derby. Standing just 5ft 2in tall, with bowed legs, a strong and sturdy frame, square face and aquiline nose, he kept his weight below eight stone all through his long exile.

He did so in readiness for this moment and he feels as fit and ready to ride as he had in his prime. He knows he must believe that. He cannot allow doubt to enter his mind. He must stay strong for his family and for himself. All of their futures hang on what happens in the next two hours.

As he walks past the exclusive Jockey Club stand he scans the faces. He is not disappointed. All the prominent patrons of racing are there without exception, including Lord Durham, whose personal attack on Charlie at the Gimcrack Dinner in 1887 helped to trigger Charlie's banishment in 1888.

He also sees some friends in the stand, the high profile individuals who supported him throughout his long ordeal and finally helped to get his licence back, including the Dukes of

Devonshire, Beaufort and Portland and the former prime minister, Lord Rosebery.

The Diamond Jubilee has brought another of Charlie's former loyal supporters, the Prince of Wales, and his large entourage, to Epsom. The Royal Standard had been raised at 12.30pm as he arrived at the Downs station. The Royal Enclosure now throngs with hundreds of distinguished guests from across the Empire, here to celebrate the Jubilee, with their gaily coloured turbans and priceless jewels lending light and brilliance to the scene.

As the mist over the Downs lifts, the racecourse is revealed in all its beauty. A fearsome thunderstorm the night before, with "thunder and lightning and rain like waterspouts", has laid the summer dust and the famous course is ready. The overnight rain means the going for the horses should be near perfect. The cloud cover on the windless day is keeping the sun from making it too hot.

The Epsom Hill, opposite the Jockey Club stand, is packed with humanity. The crowds of racegoers have made their way by every conceivable form of transport – on foot, in coaches, carts, cabs, charabancs and carriages – along the roads lined with blooming chestnuts and double blossomed redthorn. It is the one day on which social classes mix, with the exception of those allowed into the exclusive stands, and the high and low born largely forget the distinctions of rank for a day.

The crowds have lunched on pig's trotters, sandwiches, stewed eels, fried fish and hard boiled eggs as they wait for the big race. Among the booths two dozen tipsters guarantee the winner in every race. There are many tempting forms of entertainment, with farces and tragedies, boxing matches and magic tricks, being performed every few feet. The crowds can choose between the swing boats, shooting galleries, coconut shies and "tricky manipulators of cards" or they can watch the Mysterious People and the Circus of Varieties, outside which two pretty children treat onlookers to a dancing exhibition. The novelties in 1897 include the Elephant Dwarf Man from Indiana, America and the popular African Jungle – a novel shooting gallery with model lions and other exotic animals on a revolving target. Few manage to score a bull's-eye.

Right up to Tattenham Corner and beyond, people and carriages line the rails and the officials start clearing the course.

They are all there to see Charles Wood triumph – or fail. If he fails, there will be no mercy, no further come-backs. He'll be finished as a jockey.

Charles Wood by Liberio Prosperi, Vanity Fair

CHAPTER TWO

Unfortunate Beginnings

5 Henry's Place, Hull on November 21st, 1854

Throughout his life, Charlie Wood rarely referred to his childhood, deliberately keeping his birthdate shrouded in secrecy. It soon became clear that only his mother Rose, buried deep in his past, could tell the one story he worked hard all his life to keep secret, the story of his birth.

As he started to make his name as a jockey, the interest in his childhood would have grown. Biographies of his great friend and rival, the most famous jockey of that era, Fred Archer, are full of his childhood, his family history and his respected parents. The biographies of his life note that Archer's father, William Archer, won the Grand National and his mother "was aristocratic-looking". From an early age, Archer was destined to be a jockey and, as his fame grew, his mother kept copies of his birth certificate to send out to anyone enquiring about his age.

During Charlie's life, there are few references to parents or siblings and definitely no birth certificate. With good reason. The circumstances of his birth could not have been more different. It is the thread that runs through his life story and, in the late 19th century, almost certainly played a part in the harsh treatment dealt out to him by the aristocratic members of the Jockey Club.

It took a little detective work to find his birthplace and, more particularly, date of birth. He avoided making any reference to it himself and, when asked when he was born for censuses, his answers ranged from 1854 to 1856. In the few interviews he gave about his life, he always skimmed over his childhood.

About the only circumstance he would admit to was that he had been born in the Yorkshire seaport of Hull in the middle of the 19th century.

Hull sits on the northern bank of the Humber estuary, at the point where the River Hull meets the estuary, flowing down from the Yorkshire Wolds to the North Sea. At that time the seaport was famous for its fishing industry, building on its status as a whaling port. It also had a prosperous ship building industry and specialised in the import and export of grain and timber.

During the 19th century Hull burst out of its medieval walls as it went through a period of rapid growth, fuelled in part by the dramatic increase in international trade during the first half of the century.

Despite Charlie's best efforts, it is clear that his origin was known and whispered about. The *Sporting Life* in January 1889, in an article entitled 'A Sketch of this Famous Jockey's Career', went further. By that time Charlie's troubles had well and truly begun and the *Sporting Life's* sketch would have sent shivers down his spine – there, in print, was his true birthdate:

> "At this particular time... in the Yorkshire seaport town Hull... resided Master Charles Wood, in an unpretentious little house which spans Brunswick Place. He was then only 12 years of age, having been born on November 21, 1854, but it was quite time that Master Charlie Wood be launched on the world, so the question was asked 'What shall we do with our boy?'"

The article continued: "Now, the juvenile Wood was of a very diminutive size for his age, but possessed strength and coolness, so it came to pass that after careful deliberation the youth's lot in life was cast, and it was determined by his guardians that he should follow the pursuits of a jockey – providing, of course, the development of his form should not upset their calculations."[1]

It seemed a deliberate use of the term 'guardians' rather than 'parents' or 'family'. In 1834 the Poor Law set up boards of guardians to administer the workhouses and help children abandoned into poverty. Was that loaded word used to drop a heavy hint as to Charles's origins? Would his birthdate finally reveal the truth?

The envelope containing his birth certificate was handed over the counter at the Hull History Centre. It showed that a Charles Wood was indeed born on November 21st, 1854, at 5, Henry's Place, Great Passage Street, in the Myton District of Hull. His mother was Rose Wood, aged 16. Rose signed the certificate with her mark, an X. Rose did not name a father. Charlie was illegitimate.

Rose Wood had gone into labour in one of the worst slums in Hull - Henry's Place was a typical courtyard dwelling in the Myton district to the west of the main dockland area.

The narrow, confined courtyard was accessed via a tunnel through the terrace of houses lining Great Passage Street and it backed onto a large brewery. The tunnels were narrow and dark and the courtyards were crammed with small terraced housing.

The houses were often three storeys high, with walls only one brick thick. They were damp and cold in winter. Deaths from building collapses were common, and crime and disease were rife. Exploitative landlords squeezed as many families into the unsanitary, unsafe properties as they could, with reports at the time of Charlie's birth of nearly 40 people in one house. As Hull's population exploded from 22,000 at the start of the

---

[1] Sporting Life, January 26th, 1889

century to 239,000 by 1901, it led to ever more crowded and filthy housing conditions for the majority of its working class residents.

A courtyard dwelling in Hull, courtesy of the Hull History Centre

The pressure for improvements in living conditions in Hull's slums increased in 1849, five years before Charlie was born, when a cholera epidemic killed 1,863 people – one in 43 of the population. In just six weeks, 583 people died in the Myton district alone, the centre of the outbreak.

The low rent courtyard housing was not subject to any building regulation at that time and the *Hull Advertiser*, on July 13th 1849, went on the attack. "No steps have been taken to arrest the progress of this social evil, which has its origin in the cupidity of retired tradesmen, and of persons of small capital who want to realise fifty per cent on money partially borrowed upon a mortgage of the wretched tenements."

In 1854, the year of Charlie's birth, the Kingston upon Hull Bill was finally passed in Parliament. The new law outlawed tunnels, required that courtyards be widened and that builders used better construction materials and built thicker walls. It also abolished the exemption from paying rates for street lighting and cleaning enjoyed by the landlords of houses let for an annual rent of less than £6, which had acted as an incentive to build small, cheap housing and cram it full of tenants.[2]

Charlie was illegitimate, an ill-begotten bastard. In the 1850s that would stigmatise a child for its whole life. In the 19th century, the assize records show that half of all murder victims were babies – the shame was so great that mothers sometimes killed their new borns. Until 1927, the property of a bastard who died without a spouse or legitimate issue reverted to the crown. In the 1850s, an illegitimate child could not inherit. Even today, a bastard child cannot succeed to or transmit a right to any dignity or title.

In the 19th century hypocrisy was rife. Royal bastards and high born bastards might still be allowed into 'society' but not a child born out of wedlock in the slums of Hull.

The baby Charlie was simply 'Charles Wood, bastard of Rose Wood'. If the father could not be made to marry the 'deceived' maiden, he could be made to indemnify the guardians from future costs through a Bastardy Bond. Under the Poor Laws, the mother of a bastard child could apply to the Justices in Petty Sessions for a maintenance order against the father. The maximum amount she might receive after the birth was two shillings and sixpence a week.

Those records did not survive in Hull, but the threat of such an order sometimes brought the father to the altar and that might have been the case with Rose. Six months after Charlie's birth, on March 6th, 1855, at St Stephen's Church in the Parish of Holy Trinity in Kingston upon Hull, a 17-year-old Rose Wood married

---

[2] Court Housing in Kingston Upon Hull, CA Forster, 1972

the 22-year-old John Henry Chillis, a fisherman. The couple were listed as living together at Little Queen Street. Neither John Henry nor Rose could write and both signed with their mark X in the presence of Rose's younger sister, Harriet Wood. Some of Little Queen Street still exists today, in the commercial district of Hull, close to where 5, Henry's Place once stood.

John Henry Chillis's father, William, was listed as a stone mason, but John Henry disappears from the records.

There are, however, a few traces of the infant Charles from this point on. He came from an extensive family with a respectable trade in Hull. His grandfather, William Wood, was a butcher, from a family of butchers. William Wood married Elizabeth (formerly Blenkin) and, by the 1851 census, they had five children at home, including Rose. Their eldest child, Thomas, was away learning his trade as an apprentice butcher. A letter to the *Hull Daily Mail* on February 16th 1937 made it clear Thomas was Charlie's uncle.

Rose is later recorded, in the 1861 census, visiting Thomas, then living on Chestnut Street, with a six-year-old Charles Chillis. In that census record he is listed as having two siblings – John Thomas Chillis, born in 1857, and Harriet Chillis, born in 1860. They are absent from the recorded later life of Charles Wood, but a John Thomas Chillis became a stone mason, and is shown in the 1911 census as living with his wife, Priscilla and six children at 22, Temple Street, Hull.

Charlie later dropped his father's surname and worked hard to keep his illegitimate status hidden. When he married Ellen Hills in 1875, he put his father down as a 'Captain Wood', the first and only time he appears in the archive.

When Charlie was at the peak of his career and the attack on his reputation was building momentum, a few references started to appear suggesting he had Jewish blood. *The Referee*, on

December 5th 1886, sneered: "The great Mr Charles Wood, accomplished and pernicious, a Hebrew in whom are plenty of pieces but no guile, gave one of the meanest displays in the saddle ever on view."

The *Evening Star* in Australia later picked up the reference: "Wood, the jockey, is a Hebrew by birth, which accounts for his 'saving' propensities. He boasted to a lot of friends the other day that he had settled £25,000 [equivalent to £3 million in 2018] on each of his three children, besides settling a large sum on 'the missus.'"[3] After he lost his jockey licence in 1887, the *Evening Star* ran an article speculating over whether Australia would open her arms to the "wealthy little Hebrew".

The *Vanity Fair* series of cartoons on jockeys and owners generally depicts each subject in a charming light, but the one on Charlie (see page 8) is striking in its attempt to make him look shifty, with a swarthy complexion and large nose.

Class lines were clearly drawn in society in the 19th century. The aristocracy dominated racing. They ran the self-appointed governing body, the Jockey Club and – especially in flat racing – owned most of the horses. They stood as masters to their servants, the trainers, jockeys and stable boys who looked after their horses. They were the masters, socially and in law. Even today the aristocracy judge connections on their breeding. Back in the 19th century they were ruthless on the issue.

At the point the Jockey Club launched its direct attack on Charlie, it was faced with the prospect of a bastard being Champion Jockey for many years. The persecution of Jews was also commonplace at that time. The references to Hebrew may have been intended to insult Charlie. But they may also have

---

[3] Evening Star, February 5th, 1887

helped the Jockey Club to decide it had licence, in its view, to single him out for exceptionally harsh treatment.

With these burdens to carry through his life, his rise to wealth and fame was all the more exceptional. And the subsequent attack on his reputation, perhaps, all the more predictable.

CHAPTER THREE

Derby Day, 1897

The trainer gets wind of a plan to nobble his horse

Charlie is making his way to the weighing room. It is just as well that he does not know of the dangers Galtee More is facing as he is brought to join him on the course.

MR. DARLING, THE TRAINER OF GALTEE MORE.

The Illustrated Sporting and Dramatic News
© Illustrated London News Ltd/Mary Evans

Before the race the first job of Galtee More's trainer is to get the colt fit enough to have a chance of victory, without any injuries on the way. His second is to keep the horse safe from those who would like to undermine that chance of victory. Huge sums of money will be won or lost on the result, and the gamble can be made a little more certain if horses could be stopped from running well, especially the likely favourite.

In the run-up to today's big race, Darling had got wind of a plan to nobble Galtee More. He quickly found a huge dog – a Newfoundland and retriever cross – to guard the colt day and night. In his memoirs, he says the dog turned out to be a highly intelligent beast: "I placed him in the passage outside [Galtee More's] box (on a mat) one night, and he seemed to know exactly what was required of him. He went there without any persuasion afterwards."[4]

The journey from Darling's yard in Beckhampton in Wiltshire to Epsom two days earlier had also tested the endurance of his valuable charge. The trainer had travelled with the horse by train. "We were shunted at Wimbledon (and there was, I should think, about £60,000 [£7.6m] worth of horseflesh on the train), and [we] were kept there for the best part of an hour in the broiling sun."

When they finally arrived at Epsom Station, Darling and Galtee More were met by a huge crowd wanting to get an early view of the horse, and he hired two policemen standing outside the station to walk at the front and rear of his string to keep them at bay. He followed in his carriage, with the unruly crowd following behind. The procession made its slow way to the stables at The Warren in Epsom, which Darling had selected as his base for the duration of the race meeting.

In his account, Darling says Galtee More was the most charming horse to deal with and was not easily upset. This will stand him in good stead on the day of the race, when worse dangers will threaten.

By 7.30pm on the evening of their arrival, Galtee More had eaten his dinner and Darling had shut him up for the night.

---

[4] Sam Darling's Reminiscences, 1904

Before turning in himself, he decided to: "Go and have another peep at him, and my men who were also there as they were sleeping with him."

As he lit the lanterns, he found the stable alive with rats. "Galtee More's manger was almost black with them, and they ran all over the grooms – Harry and Ted Pearce – during the night."[5]

Undisturbed, on the morning of the race Galtee More enjoyed half a feed of plain oats before going out for a five furlong gallop, with another feed when he came back in.

Neither Galtee More's owner or trainer has yet won the Epsom Derby and this could be their year. They have a horse more than good enough to challenge for the one race all breeders, trainers and owners dream of winning.

Which makes their decision to spurn the leading jockeys of the day and book Charlie all the more remarkable. As the news broke in January that Charlie was back, they acted within days to secure his services, and there could have been no clearer vote of their confidence in his skills as a jockey.

Galtee More's owner, John Gubbins, tells the *Pall Mall Gazette* on the morning of the race: "I have secured... one of the best jockeys that ever wore silk, and I am glad to think that it may be through my means that Wood will ride the winner of the Triple Crown - the Two Thousand [Guineas], Derby, and St Leger."

During the interview Gubbins made it clear he also had every confidence in his horse. "I think that he'll win and that he'll win easily. No man could have taken more pains with his preparation than my trainer, Darling. All through he has told me what a great colt he believed Galtee More to be; and his performances this year have shown that the merits of the colt have not been over-estimated."

---

[5] Sam Darling's Reminiscences, 1904

Darling and Gubbins have great faith in their horse and jockey, but they know, in racing, nothing is guaranteed. Eleven horses will go to the start that afternoon and all of them have a chance of victory. The Epsom course has destroyed many dreams of victory over its long history. It has a way of finding the weaknesses in a horse with its early steep climb, tight corners and long downhill run to the finish.

The reporter asks Gubbins whether he had any fears about the last part of the race, as Galtee More was thought to have a weakness downhill.

"Not at all. This recent rain has set completely at rest any doubt I had, and probably the going at Epsom will be almost without an equal... My colt is as well as he ever was in his life, if not better."[6]

As the morning draws on, Darling starts to prepare himself and his charge for the 20-minute walk from The Warren to Epsom racecourse.

---

[6] Pall Mall Gazette, June 2nd, 1897

CHAPTER FOUR

The Apprentice

I ran away from home when I was barely thirteen years of age

He may have been born in a town known for its fishing industry and be the illegitimate son of a fisherman, but the young Charlie Wood was terrified of the sea and was always seasick. A lifetime working on the trawlers was not open to him.

As he was extremely small and lightweight for his age, racing was a clear option. The only way to make a start was to secure an apprenticeship with a racehorse trainer. Boys were in high demand to care for the horses, with one lad for every one or, at most, two horses in training in each yard. It meant a tough life of servitude, but in their hearts they each carried the dream of becoming a jockey and winning the Derby.

The 1860s were a good time to be looking for work in racing as the sport had grown to become the national obsession.

Charlie's sketchy family history shows no direct connection to horse racing and just how and when he started his search for an apprenticeship in racing is hidden in the same fog of misinformation he used to deflect questions about his early years.

There were racecourses and racing stables across the country, not least because the main method of transporting horses was by walking or riding them to the races. They were often ridden by the jockey with his racing saddle strapped around his waist. The racecourses were usually on land owned by the local aristocracy. They would use the meetings to entertain friends and enhance their social status, displaying themselves as leading members of society with processions similar to the royal procession up the course at Royal Ascot that still happens today. The railways only started to make it possible to transport horses around the country from the 1840s.

Charlie had his first stroke of fortune when he secured an apprentice at Joseph Dawson's yard in Newmarket. Dawson was one of the leading trainers at that time. During an interview published in the *Stroud Advertiser*, in the spring of 1887, he was asked when he started with Dawson. Charlie was with his wife Ellen and his son and three daughters at their winter house in Brighton. He was at the height of his powers and about to start the season when he would finally become champion jockey. Faced with a direct question, the jockey, who could recall in great detail the running of most of his races, immediately started to prevaricate.

> "You ask me when I first went to Mr Joseph Dawson. Well, that requires a bit of thinking; let me see, I rode and won on Thuringian Prince for the Royal Hunt Cup, in 1875. Thuringian Prince was a good horse. I rode the winner of the Brocklesby Stakes the same year. I won the Newmarket Handicap on Lydon in 1874."[7]

It was as if he was trying to get some verifiable dates in his mind before addressing the question.

> "Let me see, yes, I ran away from home when I was barely thirteen years of age (I was born in Hull, Yorkshire), when I weighed only 3st 9lb, and for a very short time was with Mr L'Anson, father of our current starter, Mr Bob L'Anson, at Mickleham."

---

[7] Stroud Advertiser, February 11th, 1887

When he finally got around to setting a date for his start at Dawson's, he said he secured an apprenticeship in 1870 and was indentured to him for seven years.

However, he was born in November 1854. The 1871 census lists him as one of 31 stable lads at Dawson's yard, with ages ranging from 12 to 25 years. Under the stern watch of his then master and mentor he gave his true year of birth and is listed as aged 16. The best estimate is that he arrived in Newmarket somewhere between 1864, when he was nine, and 1866 when he was aged 11, after a short spell with trainer Robert L'Anson at Mickleham, near Epsom.

How he found L'Anson is not clear, but L'Anson's family had enjoyed a long connection to the Dawson family. In 1860 L'Anson's stable jockey was "R Wood", but there is no clear connection to Charlie.

The connection between L'Anson and Dawson is more clear. Born in 1818, L'Anson had travelled north as a young man to base himself in Gullane, 20 miles east of Edinburgh, with his brother William (who trained Derby winners Blair Athol and Blink Bonny).

Joseph Dawson was born in the same town in 1825. His father was the well regarded racehorse trainer George Dawson.

L'Anson had a chequered career as a trainer and a fiery temper. At the beginning of the 1860s he was a private trainer to Sidney Jacobs, with 11 stable staff. The relationship soured in 1863 when Jacobs sued his trainer for libel in a dispute over fees. L'Anson had accused him of being a thief. Before the trial L'Anson apologised and, after a short deliberation, the jury returned a verdict for Jacobs, setting damages at one farthing. L'Anson was later sentenced to hard labour for pulling out part of a man's beard during an argument on a train. The sentence, the judge noted, clearly surprised the trainer. In 1864 he was warned off for two years after giving his 13-year-old son, Robert jnr (who would go on to become a leading steeplechase jockey), instructions "not to win" on a horse called Telscomb, following an order by the horse's owner. If Charlie arrived at L'Anson's yard in 1864 at the age of nine, just as the trainer was losing his licence, it would explain his quick move on to Newmarket.

When Charlie arrived at Dawson's yard, the trainer signed him up to a seven year apprenticeship, when the normal period was five years. In 1868, Fred Archer also made his way to Newmarket to start an apprenticeship with Joseph Dawson's brother, Mathew. Archer was 11, and he signed up for a five year apprenticeship, to finish when he was 16. If Charlie did arrive at Joseph's aged nine, a seven-year agreement would also take him to 16.

When asked, in 1887, why Joseph signed him up for seven years, Charlie had claimed: "Well, at that time seven years was the general period, although they do now, and I daresay did then take an apprentice for five years. You see I was a very light lad, and a trainer would keep one at my weight for seven years, whereas a heavier lad he might not care about taking as an apprentice for more than five."[8]

When and however it came about, the move was a key moment in Charlie's life. Joseph and Mathew Dawson were the leading trainers in the town and at that time it was said to be as: "Difficult to get a youngster taken into [their] establishments as to secure the promise of the next vacant berth at a successful military crammer."[9]

In the 19th century the life of a racing apprentice was hard. In law, they were servants, with few rights, and their relationship with their employer was governed by the Master and Servants

---

[8] Stroud Advertiser, February 11th, 1887
[9] The Sportsman, March 8th, 1877

Act. In the 1860s, masters prosecuted over 10,000 workers for breaches under that Act. No masters were prosecuted. At the turn of the 20th century a 15-year-old lad died at the Manton Stables in Lambourn. Trainer Tom Taylor was found to have taken part in the beatings that contributed to his death but walked away a free man. Under the Master and Servant Act, a master could not be found guilty of murdering a servant.

Charlie put his mark on a document that apprenticed him to Joseph Dawson for seven years. It no longer exists, but the agreement used by Mathew Dawson, when he recruited Archer, survived. In putting his mark, Charlie undertook to serve his master faithfully and keep his secrets and gladly obey his lawful commands. He swore not to commit "fornication nor contract matrimony during the said term" and "not play at cards or dice tables or any other unlawful games whereby his master shall have any loss."[10]

Archer was paid seven guineas in the first year – two guineas more than was normal because he came from a well-known racing family. His pay rose to 13 guineas in the last two years. Charlie came from a more troubled background and he probably started on the standard five guineas or less. On top of that, he received lodging, food and drink and a new hat, coat and waistcoat each year.

He was there to learn the "Art of a Jockey and Trainer of Racehorses." One of the tangible benefits he also received was an education. Mathew and Joseph had benefited from a good education and both ran evening schools for their lads. There is no record of how Joseph's school ran, but Mathew had a schoolmaster teach during the week and on Sunday morning and evening his wife taught reading and prayers, and led the singing. A member of the family would stand with slices of cake for the

[10] Fred Archer: his life and times, John Welcome, 1967

boys as they filed out, their inducement to attend the Sunday services, which were not compulsory.

Despite the best efforts of their masters, the young boys, exposed to the rough dealings in a yard, would soon have any sensitivity knocked out of them. "As a school for the acquisition of polite speech, a training stable can scarcely be recommended to parents and guardians; but this is not the fault of the trainer, any more than the petty tyrannies which schoolboys practise upon one another are the fault of the school proprietor. The amelioration of the stable boy's moral condition is a slow process due to a lack of desire to be ameliorated."[11]

Charlie had fallen on his feet and he now had to make his mark in a world where every one of his contemporaries believed they would become famous jockeys. "In Newmarket and other racing stables there are a very large number of boys employed… most of whom are apprenticed while very young to the trainers, to be taught the business of a groom. Every now and again, however, a lad of merit and mettle emerges from the crowd of his fellows and earns a reputation as a consummate horseman; but as there are more than a thousand stable-boys, and only, perhaps, some twenty jockeys of repute, it is obvious that the prizes, as in other professions, are few, and the blanks many."[12]

Joseph and Mathew Dawson were as expert in judging a young boy's potential as a jockey as they were the potential of a two-year-old thoroughbred. In Edith Humphris's biography, *The Life Of Fred Archer*, she notes:

"[Mathew] Dawson was one of the kindest and most thoughtful of masters. He was likewise a good and observant judge of the riding of his apprentices, and

---

[11] The English Turf, Theodore Cook, 1901
[12] Mirror of Turf, James Burton, 1892

had been a brilliant horseman himself in his young days. He soon began to notice the promise shown by Fred Archer, and used to say that it did not take him long to find out that he had discovered one of the greatest jockeys of all time."

Likewise with Charlie, Joseph Dawson clearly liked what he saw in his young apprentice.

"As he ran his critical eye over Wood when he entered his service, he must have thought there was material which, if properly handled, would turn out well. That he was favourably disposed to give the boy a chance is quite certain, for the tyro [novice] had not been in his stables long before he had a leg up into the saddle."[13]

---

[13] Sporting Life, January 26th, 1889

CHAPTER FIVE

Derby Day, 1897

A blue blooded racing aristocrat

As the start draws close, Galtee More bears far more than weight of the huge sums gambled on his winning. Along with the hopes of all his connections, the pride of a troubled Ireland will gallop alongside the horse and his jockey.

MR. GUBBINS, THE OWNER OF GALTEE MORE.

The Illustrated Sporting and Dramatic News
© Illustrated London News Ltd/Mary Evans

Galtee More is owned by his breeder, John Gubbins, a well-built County Limerick man with a luxurious handlebar moustache and piercing brown eyes set in a bronzed face.

A genial man, Gubbins was born with a deep love of racing and hunting but without the funds in his youth to enjoy either as he wished. But he was one of life's lucky men. Although from humble origins, he managed to keep in the good books of his childless uncle, a successful Irish distiller called Francis Wyse. Wyse lived a blameless life, with "great care and even frugality" and contrived to leave a large fortune to John Gubbins and another of his nephews. Gubbins was in America when he received the news of his inheritance and quickly returned to set about enjoying the life of a wealthy Irish gentleman.

In the early days of his return, he dedicated his life to race riding and hunting, and his house was full of mementoes of his successful days as jockey and passionate hunter. Pride of place is given to a fox brush on a shield, with an inscription saying it was presented by the Belvoir huntsman, Frank Gillard, in memory of a brilliant 45-minute run on December 2nd, 1887.

The rise of Irish nationalism, however, set in train events that would lead to this fateful Derby. Gubbins was Master of the Limerick Hunt until 1882, when a meet was stopped by large groups of nationalists from the Irish National Land League throwing sticks and stones at the hounds. The Land League's primary aim was to remove the absentee English landlords and give the land back to the tenants who worked it. Gubbins shouted: "For God's sake leave the hounds alone; I'd rather you threw stones at me!" He took the hunt home and never hunted in Ireland again.

From that day, he focused on breeding thoroughbreds in Ireland and training them in England. His beloved Buree and Knockany studs were in the Golden Vale of County Limerick, in the shadow of the Galtee Mountains, and such was his passion for racing and his studs he left instructions on his death: "As I aspired to breed fast horses please see that my hearse is pulled at speed on my final journey."

In 1893 he moved his string of horses from Telscombe in Sussex to Sam Darling, who trained at Beckhampton in Wiltshire.

His first major win came a year later in 1894 when his home-bred Blairfinde, out of a mean and moody mare Morganette, won the Irish Derby. He named the foal he bred from the same mare the year of the Irish win after the tallest peak in the Galtee range, the *Geal Tigh Mor*.

Galtee More is a blue-blooded racing aristocrat in his own right. He bears the blood of the Arabians in his veins and epitomises the romance of the thoroughbred.

He is descended from Scham, the Godolphin Arabian. The way Scham's arrived in England was the stuff of legends, and a romantic version of the story made its way into the papers as the Derby approached.[14]

In 1730, it was said that the Bey of Tunis, monarch of Tunisia and vassal of the Grand Turk of the Ottoman Empire, sent eight pure-blooded barbs as a gift to Louis XV of France. The most beautiful of the eight was Scham, a bay high crested stallion of four years, attended by his own groom, Agba the Moor. A small embroidered bag hung around the stallion's neck recording his regal lineage.

The king and his court were far too busy womanising and hunting to care much for the gift, and the magnificent stallion was sold to a brutal carter in Paris. The winter of 1732 was bitter, and the stallion would have died but for the devoted care of Agba, who never left him. One winter's day, pulling a load of bricks up the hill from the Rue Dauphine to the Pont Neuf,

---

[14] Derby Mercury, June 9th, 1897

Scham collapsed from exhaustion. The carter's attempts to beat him back to his feet attracted the attention of an English Quaker, Edward Coke, who immediately bought the horse, paying 15 Louis for him. He took Scham and Agba to England where the stallion soon recovered.

On his death in 1733, Coke bequeathed the stallion to Mr Williams of the St James's Coffee House, who sold him on to Lord Godolphin, and Scham and Agba found themselves at the Earl's stud farm on the Gog Magog Hills of Cambridgeshire.

To Agba's horror, Scham had been bought as a teaser. The stud stallion Hobgoblin was awaiting a mare called Roxana and Scham was led into the covering paddock to make sure she was ready to be claimed by Hobgoblin. Scham was then led away and shut up in his box, where he screamed and kicked with such fury that his devoted groom slipped the bar and Scham charged back to the paddock, making straight for his rival. The two stallions fought, and Hobgoblin's size and weight at first kept his rival down, but then Scham broke free. Wheeling round, he delivered a battery of kicks on the ribs of Hobgoblin and the great white stallion was vanquished. Scham claimed his prize.

The Godolphin Arabian went on to cover many more mares and his bloodline played a major role in the creation of the modern thoroughbred.

Despite his excellent breeding, Galtee More was not Gubbins's personal favourite from that year's foals, but luckily for Sam Darling and Charlie, the stud manager Mike Burns stood up for the big bay colt and he was sent over to Darling as a two year old.

Today Galtee More has to show whether that early faith in him was justified.

J. DAWSON.   Copyright—H. & R., & A. & S., Ld

CHAPTER SIX

The Mentor

There had never been in Newmarket a trainer more beloved and respected

Joining Joseph Dawson's yard was the key to Charlie's future success. The Scottish trainer had arrived in Newmarket in 1859 and through the 1860s he revolutionised the way racehorses were trained, as well as the status of trainers and jockeys. When he first arrived in the Suffolk town, it was almost finished as a racing centre. Trainers had lost faith in its racing facilities, declaring its gallops to "adamantine" [hard], and owners increasingly declined to send their horses there.

> "It was feared that the sun which had shone so brightly over the gay scenes of sport on the classic Heath had set, to rise no more... Suddenly, however, there came an unexpected revolution... Everything changed as if by magic, and the inhabitants of Newmarket became once more happy and prosperous. Mr Joseph Dawson brought Lord Stamford's horses to be trained there, and in 1861 Diophantus secured the Two Thousand Guineas. From that time the land of the Heath resumed its former prosperity."[15]

Dawson came with the horses of his master, Lord Stamford, to set up a yard at Heath House in Moulton Road. The majority of trainers and jockeys, especially in aristocratic Newmarket, made their living in service to their masters, earning a wage

---

[15] Sporting Life, January 26th, 1889

regardless of the number of horses in training. The majority of trainers were simply 'training grooms', the jockeys for the most part lads who lived with them. As *Badminton Racing* reported at the time: "Few of either class betted to any extent, or owned horses at all. They were employed at fixed salaries by the gentlemen who patronised the turf."[16]

Dawson's father, George Dawson, had been a well-respected and independent trainer, based at Stamford Hall, Gullane, East Lothian, about 20 miles east of Edinburgh. Joseph was the thirteenth child of 17, born in December 1825. His brother Mathew, from whom he was inseparable throughout his life and who would also rise to be one of the country's leading trainers, was five years older. George Dawson was said to be a: "Most upright, skilful and industrious trainer, and also a rigid disciplinarian in the education and management of his sons and daughters."[17] If any got into mischief he was quick to beat them with the *tawse*, a strip of leather, with one end split into a number of tails. (Its use was finally abolished in the 1980s in Scotland.)

Between them, four of his sons, Thomas, Mathew, Joseph and John, went on to win 42 classic races, including nine Derbys. Their success was credited in part to the superior education they received in Scotland. Their schoolmaster, Mr Thomson, had been a medical student but found he could not stand the sight of blood and settled as a teacher in Gullane from 1812 until his death in 1872. As a result, the Dawson children could all read and write and they placed a high value on a good education, which they brought to the management of their yards by running schools for their lads.

---

[16] Badminton Library: Racing and Steeplechasing, Earl of Suffolk and Berkshire and WG Craven, 1887
[17] The Life of Mathew Dawson, Edith Humphris, 1928

Training started to develop as a business, with public trainers, during the 19th century and Newmarket emerged early because of its royal connections. Yorkshire was not too far behind due to its early lead in racehorse breeding.

Good rail connections became key in the mid 19th century, and racecourses without nearby stations began to close. Newmarket's struggle to survive as a racing centre in the 1850s was in part because the northern horses started to dominate the classics after transporting horses south became easier. Its resurgence started when the aristocratic northern owners started to move to London and brought their horses south and was consolidated after Joseph Dawson moved there.

From 1848 to 1898, Newmarket grew from 23 important yards to 40. Meanwhile Gullane went from five yards in 1858 to none in 1888, although it may have still had smaller yards in operation.[18]

The Dawson family's invasion of the English racing establishment reflected those changes, starting with the eldest son, Tom, who set himself up as a public trainer at Breconsgill Stables, Middleham, Yorkshire, in 1830.

In the early days, Tom's yard was run alongside his father's, and many of their Scottish patrons divided their horses between the two. The family found it needed a more southern outpost because, although there are examples of 'vanning' horses (moving them in covered horse drawn carts), as early as the 1830s, the usual way to transport horses before the railways was on foot, which sometimes meant walking 25 miles in a day. It was a long and arduous journey for Scottish horses entered into the increasingly popular big races in the south.

In 1840 Mathew Dawson undertook the journey from the "Land o'Cakes" to Epsom for the Derby. He was in charge of

---

[18] Nineteenth Century Racehorse Stables in their Rural Setting: a Social and Economic Study, Mike Huggins, 1996, Cambridge University Press

Pathfinder, one of the first horses he trained in his own name. "His journey was performed principally by road... On their way southward the horse and his custodian stopped at Catterick Bridge, where Pathfinder, ridden by George Nelson, won a match for 300 sovereigns against Mr Meiklam's Remedy, ridden by Tommy Lye."[19] Pathfinder finished last in the Derby, 200 yards behind the second last horse.

Tom Dawson was known as 'King o't'Moor' to his neighbours, and 'Dangerous Dawson' to his competitors. He was also the inspiration for many of his good friend John Frederick Herring's paintings. Herring used to wander about Dawson's grounds at Middleham, painting any horse that caught his eye. He gave many of the paintings to his friend.

Tom Dawson started the development of a very different way to train horses, which Joseph Dawson then brought to Newmarket:

> "Mr Thomas Dawson of Middleham was the originator of the improved system of training thoroughbreds. He was the first to see the fallacies of the old method, and to act upon his own well considered opinion. He did away with the drenchings, profuse sweatings and short supplies of water, introducing in their stead plenty of good oats and hard work. Mr Mathew Dawson to this day often quotes 'my brother Tom' as an oracle on horseflesh, and the thanks of owners are justly due to him for the radical and salutary change he has effected in the training world."[20]

---

[19] The Life Of Fred Archer, Edith Humphris, 1934
[20] Badminton Library: Racing and Steeplechasing, Earl of Suffolk and Berkshire and WG Craven, 1887

As a result, Tom Dawson won five classics, including the Derby with Ellington in 1856. The Derby win netted him £25,000 [£2.6m] – which he promptly left in a hat box on the train home. He advertised for its return saying it contained nothing of interest except to the owner and it was returned unopened.

Because of the distance and difficulty of transporting horses, he started to get the best of the Scottish horses staying in his yard. Mathew Dawson later joined his brother as head lad before returning to Scotland to work with his father until George's death in 1846, an event that triggered the eventual migration of brothers Mathew, John and Joseph to Newmarket.

Joseph moved to Tom's yard in 1847, first working for his brother and then training for WS Davidson. In August 1852 he married Harriet Briggs, whose uncle John Fobert had trained the Flying Dutchman to win the Derby in 1849. Harriet was a strong personality and, according to his niece Jean Neale, Joseph was always in awe of her.

In 1853 the couple moved to East Isley in Berkshire. By 1858, he was training there for the Earl of Stamford and Warrington and, in 1859, he moved with Stamford's horses to Heath House in Newmarket.

Mathew Dawson stayed on in Scotland for a year after his father's death, before finding himself forced to leave Gullane and move south. At the time he blamed it on the decline of horse racing in Scotland, the depreciation in the value of bloodstock and "the foreign market being shut up by the disturbances on the Continent."[21]

When he first came south he trained mostly for Lord John Scott, dividing his time between Rugby, Newmarket and

---

[21] Badminton Library: Racing and Steeplechasing, Earl of Suffolk and Berkshire and WG Craven, 1887

Compton in Berkshire. When Scott decided to retire from racing, Mathew did not waste time. He went to London to find James Merry, the Glasgow-based ironmaster who had had horses in training with his father in Scotland. After tracking him down on Bond Street, he asked him to buy Scott's stud of horses. Merry agreed and soon Mathew was settled at Russell Park near Lambourn with horses that would establish his reputation.

As his private trainer, Mathew was Merry's servant, and Merry paid him £250 [£33,000] a year. The position came with a free house, but Mathew had to buy his own coal. Merry met the cost of keeping the horses and his trainer received nothing extra per horse.

When Joseph Dawson arrived in Newmarket he was still in service to Stamford, and he quickly set a new standard in the way he ran Heath House stables. The *Leicestershire Mercury* visited the yard in 1862.

"Since his sojourn at Newmarket, and the exclusive management of his stud by [Joseph] Dawson, there have, of course, been the occasional victories or defeats attendant upon the pursuit. But there can be little doubt that, if racing is to be entered upon at all, it should be on the scale that we see it here. In everything that Lord Stamford does he pursues his object with a fixed steadiness of purpose and perfection of execution which is a marked phase of his character. In pursuance of this principle there have been built for him by Mr. Weatherby, at the back of his trainer's house, a handsome court-yard containing 28 stalls and boxes, tenanted by just so many horses, whose general appearance, condition, and care reflect the very highest credit upon Mr Dawson."[22]

---

[22] Leicestershire Mercury, June 7th, 1862

Joseph Dawson's relationship with Stamford was not easy. The Earl had succeeded to his title and estates at a young age and was enormously wealthy, even by the standards of the time. The estates were not entailed and there was something in the young man's character that clearly worried his relations, leading his uncle to try to get him to sign an oath to marry within his class. The uncle was right to be worried as Stamford refused and then married for love. Victorian society did not welcome the beautiful new wife of the 7th Earl of Stamford and Warrington, because Catherine Cox had previously earned her living as a daring bareback horse rider in Astley's circus.

As the aristocracy would later be ruthless with Charlie when he dared to rise above his class, so they were with the new Lady Stamford. When the couple arrived home after the wedding, the bell ringers at the nearby village of Bowdon defied the priest and church wardens and began to ring a special welcoming peal, for which they expected a handsome tip. The wardens broke down the door to silence the bells.

The couple had to weather many bruising snubs, including Queen Victoria's refusal to sit in an adjoining box at the opera. They were also deeply upset by the public humiliation they endured during their visit to Knutsford races in 1855, when Lady Stamford was greeted by a barricade of turned backs and raised parasols and people hissed "strumpet" as she passed. Stamford, however, was protected from such rebuffs by his enormous wealth. He and his wife loved racing and went on to invest heavily in their horses. As Dawson learnt early in their relationship, the Earl also bet heavily.

"No story was more frequently on Joseph Dawson's lips than one which related that almost the first two year old brought out for Lord Stamford was a filly — her name, we think, was Cellina — engaged in the Althorp

Park Stakes. Just as the flag was about fall, Lord Stamford told his trainer, who was quite unnerved by the communication, that he had backed the filly almost at evens against the field, for £10,000 [£1.2m]. Beautifully ridden by Edwards the mare just won by a head."[23]

Dawson was starting to hone his skills as a trainer and, with the assistance of Lady Stamford, he set about looking after the many young boys in his care.

"Order and regularity, cleanliness, obedience, and civility are the watchwords of the stable. The mere grooming and attention is, of course, first-rate. It is so elsewhere; but it is a great piece of management to see the boys, each to his own horse, with his brushes, combs, sponges, &c., arranged at the foot of the stall on a clean linen cloth at half-past six, so cleanly, tidily dressed, civil, and attentive – in a word, so manifestly cared for, not only physically, but morally – that it is a most valuable comparison to be able to make with the stables of so many noblemen and gentlemen engaged in the same pursuits here and elsewhere. Regularity of hours and attention to the health and behaviour of these lads affords them a pleasing guarantee that they are working under a master who has their real good at heart, and whose influence may keep them on the right road amidst trials and temptations where higher motives would fail."[24]

---

[23] Brierley Hill Stourbridge Kidderminster and Dudley News, January 6th, 1883
[24] Brierley Hill Stourbridge Kidderminster and Dudley News, January 6th, 1883

With the arrival of Joseph Dawson, the lives of racehorses in Newmarket took a dramatic turn for the better as he quickly adopted and refined his brother Tom's methods of feeding and training. They soon started to be treated with the same care and attention that today's top thoroughbreds enjoy. Hard as it is to believe, the tradition in the town to that point was to lock the horses in their stables, drench them and heat the stables to make them sweat. They were also, as part of their regime, sometimes galloped in rugs. A regular writer on racing, Sir Francis Lawley, commented in the *Australian* on the way horses were over trained before Joseph Dawson.

"It was the fashion to sweat a horse, whether gross or light, at least once a week, and in some cases three times in a fortnight… When I was a youngster I knew Mr John Scott, of Malton, who was a great advocate of sweating, and many a horse of his have I ridden in a sweating gallop round Little London (a circular tan track) three or four times, and up the hill to the rubbing-house, where the horse was stripped and rubbed down by two men, and afterwards given a smart gallop of five furlongs or three-quarters of a mile."[25]

The trainers at that time believed that the thinner the horse, the fitter it was. John George Witt wrote in his memoir *The Three Villages* in 1904: "In my recollection Newmarket horses came to the post looking like towel-horses, skeletons on shaky legs." He tells the story of an owner who went to see his horses to find they were lame in one leg. The trainer said they were not fit to try. He went a month later and they were lame in two legs, and the trainer said they were nearly fit. The owner went a month later

---

[25] The Australian, September 22nd, 1894

and they were lame on three legs and the trainer declared, "Now, my Lord, they are all just fit to try."[26]

Along with the sweating regimes, trainers up to that point took little or no care of their young stock and they often arrived weak and poorly grown to be trained as two-year-olds. Sensing an opportunity, Dawson started to feed his youngsters the best oats from the Carse O'Gowrie in Scotland along with rich Jersey milk, leading the *Badminton Library* to report that it was said of him: "That he would give his horses gold if he thought they would eat it, and that it would do them good."[27]

The weanlings in the paddocks behind Bedford Lodge started to look like yearlings well before they reached their first birthday. As they reached their second year they were regularly galloped on Newmarket Heath without rugs to get them properly fit, leaving them rippling with muscle, unlike their skinny opposition. Joseph soon became legendary, especially for his preparation of his two-year-olds.

However, his radical approach was initially met with considerable resistance. Horse people are nothing if not lovers of tradition. Reports at the time said he was the laughing stock of Newmarket, until the success enjoyed by his stable changed derision to imitation. Lawley notes: "Well do I recollect when Mr Joseph Dawson first went to train at Newmarket how he was laughed at and ridiculed for not sweating his horses as others did. But he outlived all the ridicule, and had the satisfaction of seeing his own method come into vogue long before he died. No one won more races or placed their horses better than he did and it was a lucky day for Lord Stamford when he selected him for his private trainer." John George Witt agreed, saying the extraordinary prosperity of the town could be clearly dated from

---

[26] The Three Villages, John George Witt, 1904
[27] Badminton Library, Racing and Steeplechasing, Earl of Suffolk and Berkshire and WG Craven, 1887

the arrival of Joseph Dawson who, with his famous brothers, taught the modern system of training. For some, however, it was all just too much:

> "On the journey to Epsom, I naturally asked Mr Bruty, who had trained in Bombay as well as Newmarket, what horse would, in his opinion, win the race. He replied, 'I do not know what will win, but I do know what will not win, and that is that brute Hermit. If he wins there is no sense or meaning in training, and I will never train a horse again as long as I live'... When Hermit passed the post an easy winner, Mr Bruty lapsed into absolute silence. He went home, sold his horses, saddlery and clothing, discharged his boys, got rid of his house and stables, shook the dust off his feet against Newmarket Heath and town, and went to Cambridge where he bought a brewery."[28]

For Charlie, the key moment in Joseph Dawson's life was his falling out with Stamford in late 1863. The *Sporting Intelligence* reported that: "Much sensation has been created in Newmarket by the movements that have lately taken place in connexion with Lord Stamford's stud. We understand that, on Monday, his lordship sent a peremptory order to Joseph Dawson, his late trainer, to deliver up every horse and all effects belonging to him."

The falling out followed the claim by Stamford that one of his horses, Limosina, must have been drugged after she had returned to the weigh-in "bathed in cold, clammy sweat," dragging her hind feet behind her, although the mare may have been exhausted by the numerous false starts that delayed the race for over an hour. The racing press started suggesting that any

---

[28] The Three Villages, John George Witt, 1904

tampering with the mare would have been impossible without the assistance of someone working for Dawson.

The relationship with Stamford may have soured, but Dawson was more than able to stand up for himself. The master and his former servant fought over everything, including who would keep the lads and the stable jockey, and they offered all sorts of competing inducements, including dinners and life-long stipends. It also led to the highly unusual spectacle of a servant suing an aristocrat for money owed. Dawson was successful and the damages allowed him to purchase Bedford Lodge in Newmarket where he set about building a stable yard that fitted with his training philosophy, including large airy boxes. Charlie later built a yard and stud farm in the town and Bedford Lodge was his model – both can still be identified by the ornate plaques with their owner's initials over the main stable block.

Trainer and owner remained at daggers drawn for some time. Three years later, in 1866, the *Sporting Life* reported that a bill has been filed in the courts by Stamford seeking to establish his right to the lease on a house and gallops. In 1861 they had been secured by Dawson while he was still employed by Stamford on a seven-year lease. The canny Scotsman had taken the lease in his own name and he remained firmly in possession after the two men parted company. Stamford claimed that even though the lease was clearly in Joseph's name, he had thought it was in his.

In 1866 Dawson found himself before an outraged Vice Chancellor Wood. The judge decided in Stamford's favour, stating that, as Dawson was only a servant of his lordship, he should award the case to the plaintiff. In doing so, he took the opportunity to pass some severe strictures on the trainer's conduct towards Stamford, one of the "most distinguished patrons of the turf." The Master of the Rolls overturned the decision in Dawson's favour and Stamford, who had come to regret the falling out, later made in effect a public apology by returning all of his horses in training to Dawson where they stayed until Dawson's death in 1880. In 1888 Charlie would also find himself facing a judge who still thought servants should know their place.

The opening of Bedford Lodge as a training yard on October 3rd, 1864 set Dawson up as a public trainer in Newmarket, and he would go on to have few equals in his profession. Within a month of leaving Stamford, he had over 50 horses in his yard. In 1866, Mathew took on Joseph's former yard at Heath House and he followed the same system of feeding and training as his brother.

> "Their manners are courteous, their stable management has passed into proverb, and their judgement of a yearling is held in as high repute as their irreproachable taste for whisky."[29]

Mathew, who was said to be a martinet over his training and was famed for the polish he put on his horses, always said he was not in the same street as his brother and he was a fool in the stable compared with Joseph.

The brothers were devoted to each other and their nephew, John Dawson, said they reminded him of the Cheeryble brothers from Charles Dickens's *Nicholas Nickleby*. Nobody could come between them, although Lord Falmouth was foolish enough to try. Mathew was by then established as a successful public trainer, and Falmouth, one of the most successful owners in the history of racing, was one of his clients. In 1870, Falmouth made the mistake of countermanding an order given to a jockey by Mathew who: "At once wrote a letter to his Lordship requesting him to remove his horses, as the confidence which ought to exist between them was evidently gone."

---

[29] Sporting Life, March 8th, 1877

Falmouth went to Joseph and asked him to take all of his horses. "My brother Mat trains for you, my Lord," replied Joseph. "I can't take your horses." "But they are leaving him," said Falmouth. "I can't have them," repeated Joseph, "but perhaps I had better speak to Mat about them."[30] Joseph made up the differences between the two and the partnership, with the help of stable jockey Fred Archer, went on to become legendary.

The two brothers stood at the vanguard of a revolution in the racing industry. Private trainers started to give way to public trainers and soon successful yards would have over 70 horses in training for a range of different owners. *The English Turf* said the change secured Newmarket's position as a centre of racing as owners started to scatter their horses amongst the public trainers there. "Newmarket is the fashionable centre, and many an aristocratic owner trains there who might be expected to entrust his horses to a trainer in his own district. With the richest men from all parts of the country concentrating at one spot, that spot may be expected to yield the best results." The popularity of the town, it said, was underpinned by the possession of a variety of fine training grounds and the eight race meetings held there during the year.

> "An owner can thus combine the two pleasures of seeing his horses at work and attendance at a pleasant first-rate meeting. He can see or hear something of the horses of his friends; he can very often arrange his trials for a race week; and if, as a regular attendant at the meetings, he has a house in or near the town, as is so customarily the case, he can see far more of his horses than he would if they were trained elsewhere in

---

[30] The Life of Mathew Dawson, Edith Humphris, 1928

the country; and some owners practically reside there all the year round."[31]

Joseph Dawson's independent status allowed him to pick and choose his owners and the jockeys he employed and, along with the growing band of public trainers, he started to favour certain jockeys to ride his owners' horses. That change in turn started to set the jockeys free, and the best of them, rather than having one employer, began to be retained by several owners or trainers through the payment of an annual fee.

Dawson suffered from poor health for most of his life, attributed to diabetes, and died aged 55 in 1880. When he died, it was said that there had never been in Newmarket a trainer more beloved and respected while: "To his brother Mathew, his senior by a few years, his loss was simply irreparable. Their love for each other was wonderful, passing the love of brothers."[32]

Sir Francis Lawley, who later wrote *The Bench and the Jockey Club* in 1889 in support of Charlie after the attack on his reputation, had known Joseph Dawson since 1853, both as a friend and trainer of one of his horses.

"As a man I might say of him ... 'a more perfect gentleman never lived.' Never have I known an individual in any station of life, more incapable of a mean, ignoble, treacherous, or ungenerous thought than Joseph Dawson... it is quite enough for me, then, that down to his dying hour – I saw him for the last time in that bed from which, I clearly foresaw he was never again destined to rise – Joseph Dawson liked, admired, and believed in Wood."[33]

---

[31] The English Turf, Theodore Cook, 1901
[32] The Life Of Fred Archer, Edith Humphris, 1934
[33] The Bench and the Jockey Club, Francis Lawley, 1889

CHAPTER SEVEN

Derby Day, 1897

I put my shoulder under this fellow and gave him a shove

As the racegoers, horses, owners and jockeys start to converge on the paddock, Galtee More sets out to walk from The Warren to the racecourse. As the big bay horse leaves the gates, two housemaids run out to blow him a kiss.

Luckily, Sam Darling decides to escort Galtee More himself, with a lad on board, and takes along his stable companion Glenmorgan to help keep him calm.

They set off in the company of John Corlett, editor of the *Sporting Times* and The Warren's ploughman, who decides to come along because he "had a dollar on".

> "Trouble, and serious trouble, only began at the very point at which, if there had been trouble, it should've ended. It was when the favourite and his escort came within the scope of the Epsom management that all the trainer's care and attention might have been – and with a bad tempered horse would have been – thrown away, and a horse valued at £30,000 [£3.8m], the chief actor in the big tough drama of the day, ruined through the neglect or want of consideration of officials."[34]

The Warren is on the far side of the racecourse, the opposite side from where most of the horses are stabled. The road is quiet and,

---

[34] A Pink 'un Remembers, JB Booth, 1937

given their route, Darling assumes that the simplest thing is for Galtee More to enter at the gate nearest to them, the gate the Derby horses will later use to leave the paddock.

When the procession, led by Glenmorgan, arrives at that first entrance they find their way barred by an implacable guard. They are forced to walk on round the perimeter to find the next gate.

As they walk, the group becomes entangled amongst all the horse drawn vehicles making their way to the race and one of the drivers starts whipping up his team. Galtee More finally loses his cool and starts to plunge.

Darling finds his difficulties compounded at this point. "I had the greatest trouble here with Galtee More for, of course, he was a stallion, and there were some mares close by, which made him very excited."

Finally they see the entrance but find their way barred by another chain. It is a simple matter to let the procession through and: "Mr Corlett with his umbrella, and myself close behind, tried to persuade the man to loose the chain and let us into the course, but the man said he did not have any orders to do so. I put my shoulder under this fellow and gave him a shove, and politely sent him into the course (to the delight of the crowd) and we got through."[35]

Unscathed, they arrive in the paddock and join John Gubbins. They find a quiet corner by a high hedge at the far end, away from the crowds starting to pour in.

To keep Galtee More calm, they walk him on a large circle with Glenmorgan while they wait for Charlie to arrive.

---

[35] Sam Darling's Reminiscences, 1914

Mary Evans Picture Library

CHAPTER EIGHT

The Golden Years

From runaway to Champion Jockey

When Sam Darling and John Gubbins secured Charlie to ride Galtee More in the horse's most important season as a three year old, their decision was not based on a whim. Ten years before, in 1887, the season before he lost his licence, Charlie had become champion jockey after standing second to Fred Archer in the championship for the preceding seven years.

Charlie won his first race in 1872 when he was 17. He remembered it well for the rest of his life, telling the *Illustrated Sporting and Dramatic News* during an interview at the start of 1887: "It was in a handicap at Newmarket, a horse called Henry V. There were only two starters, and I beat Fordham; but I expect I was on a good bit the better horse, for he always had the best of boys when it came to a finish if the horses were anything like equal."

It was a notable achievement for the rookie to beat the many times champion jockey, George Fordham, nicknamed 'The Kid' for the way he fooled the other jockeys in a race. Looking left and right Fordham would cluck and fiddle, feigning concern about his horse. His fellow jockeys, thinking they had him in difficulties, would plunge simultaneously into the ecstasies of a flogging finish, using up too much of their horses too early, only to find, with the semblance of a shake, the kidder Fordham would shoot out and canter home an easy winner.

When the *Illustrated Sporting and Dramatic News* reporter added: "And you've ridden a few winners since." Charlie smiled, "as so successful a man well may," and replied that he had been wonderfully lucky.

After that first win, Charlie continued to show promise and his master and mentor, Joseph Dawson, started to put him up more and more in public. As a result he clocked up a steady run of 27 victories during the 1873 and 1874 seasons.

Dawson was a staunch protector of his apprentice in those early years. Charlie had been given the ride on a horse that the owner thought was a dead cert, but it was well beaten and the owner complained about his riding to Dawson. He got short shrift. The angry trainer retorted that, wooden or not wooden, the owner could not expect his young protégé to win on a "dashed bad horse."

By 1874, the 19-year-old Charlie was still to achieve his full potential and he must have taken a knock when his younger rival, the 17-year-old Fred Archer, shot to the top to become champion jockey. Archer had caught the eye of Lord Falmouth, one of the leading owners at that time, and he soon rewarded Falmouth's faith in him by winning the young jockey's first classics, the 2,000 Guineas on Atlantic, followed by the 1,000 Guineas two days later on Spinaway.

Charlie often said that Archer had been the best jockey of that era. A hugely talented jockey, he is still highly regarded today, and has been the subject of several biographies. He was also a key figure in Charlie's life, a great friend and rival, and between them they dramatically changed the status of jockeys for the better.

Once he became champion jockey, Archer was never beaten to the title until his suicide 13 years later in 1886. Charlie stood second to him for seven years from 1879. But he was always some distance off Archer's tally of wins in each season.

It is clear from the contemporary commentaries that Charlie did not have Archer's desire to win at all costs. Archer, whose nickname was the 'Tinman' because of his relentless pursuit of money, would search the calendar for possible winners that he might ride. It often meant a horse running and winning that would otherwise have been left in the stable. He never left anything to chance and was always on the lookout for things that would contribute to the success of his mount. He made a practice of leaving the paddock first in order that he might reach the start before the others and get what he considered the best position. In his short career he rode 8,084 races, with 2,748 winners, more than one win every three mounts.[36]

It is hard to ignore, however, the many references to how Archer's will to win sometimes broke the hearts of the horses he rode. As Edith Humphries says in her biography of the jockey, *The Life Of Fred Archer*, the problem with Archer was that, often overwhelmed by his desire to win, he could be heavy with his whip and spurs. "Often a horse he won a hard race on never did any more racing afterwards. If any amount of flogging would help to win, Archer would be unmerciful to his horse."

In later life, Archer acknowledged that he had been hard on his horses as a young jockey.

"Archer owed his great successes partly to his consummate judgement of time and pace, partly to his daring nature. He never hesitated, for example, to take the inside of the turn at Tattenham Corner, and so come at top speed down the hill, while other jockeys, afraid of their necks, were making wide bends, and so losing lengths in the race. As to the punishment he was said to inflict on his horses, his own words uttered not many months before his death were, 'I know a few

---

[36] Illustrated Sporting and Dramatic News, November 13th, 1886

years back I was a severe rider; but I've learnt better by experience. I rarely hit a horse more than twice in a finish now, and I hardly ever have rowels to my spurs. You can hurt a horse almost as much without them – but it's bad policy to hurt them at all.'"[37]

In addition, Archer was renowned as a tyrant on the racecourse, taking every opportunity to intimidate the other jockeys. He thought nothing of attempting to put them over the rails if they had the temerity to try to overtake him.

In 1874, the year Archer became champion jockey, he rode in a race against a young jockey, William Clay, from Jevington, the village in Sussex where Charlie later settled. Clay's horse fell during the race and the jockey died from his injuries. The reports made it clear that his father, trainer William Clay, thought that the two jockeys riding either side of his son's horse were involved. One of them was the 17-year-old Archer. The inquest exonerated the jockeys and William Clay, who could not bear to be in court to hear the evidence, accepted the verdict.[38]

In another race, when his brother Charles Archer (who started as a jockey before becoming a trainer) had the cheek to try and come up inside the rails, Fred Archer promptly put him over the rails, almost breaking his neck.

In *Kings of the Turf*, William Dixon, under the pseudonym 'Thormanby', reviewed Archer's career, noting that some maintained that Archer's success was more due to good luck than good horsemanship and that at the best he was just a clever trickster, not a great master of the art of riding.

"They aver that the mere terror of his name and of his fierce, unscrupulous style of cutting down his

[37] Kings of the Turf, Thormanby (William Dixon), 1898
[38] Berkshire Chronicle, September 5th, 1874

opponents, frightened younger and more timid jockeys, and that they lost both nerve and judgement when the terrible 'Tinman' was against them. There may be some small grain of truth in these theories, which aim at disparaging Archer's merit as a jockey. But even if you allow them far more weight than they deserve, they still fall far, very far, short of reasonably accounting for Archer's marvellous triumphs in the saddle... that he was a great jockey no one, whose sense of justice is not utterly warped by prejudice, can honestly deny."[39]

The descriptions of his early style of riding – although within the rules of the time – suggest he would have fallen foul of the rules governing racing and protecting the horses from abuse that exist today. Charlie would be accused of many things later in life but not of abusing his horses.

Archer's approach may have been in part due to his size. He was tall for a flat race jockey at 5'10" and his natural weight was around 11 stone. It meant he could be a strong rider, but he continually had to starve himself to keep his weight down. He used saunas and strong laxatives to try to keep below nine stone, but often carried more weight than his rivals. Charlie, on the other hand, stopped growing when he reached 5'2" and rarely weighed over eight stone, even in his mature years.

As the 1870s progressed, Charlie may have had fewer winners than Archer, but in 1875 he started to get more widely noticed for his skills as a jockey. He was 21 years of age and becoming a popular jockey with some prominent owners, chalking up 43 wins that year. These included several high profile races, notably the Royal Hunt Cup with his mentor Joseph

---

[39] Kings of the Turf, Thormanby (William Dixon), 1898

Dawson's Thuringian Prince and the Earl Spencer's Plate with Mr Tucker's Gunner.

Charlie was also maturing. In December 1875 he married Ellen Hills, the daughter of the publican at the Lamb Hotel in Ely, Cambridgeshire. They went on to have six children, with their first child and only son, James Hills Wood, born in Newmarket in September 1876. Ellen was a good horsewoman and they shared a love of hunting.

He was also showing himself to be a loyal friend. With owner Sir George Chetwynd (who was later caught up alongside Charlie in the attack on their reputations), he helped to bring George Fordham back to racing after he had retired in 1875 and promptly lost all his money. The former champion jockey turned to gin and the pair persuaded him to abandon the drink and race again. Fordham went on to have nearly 500 more winners, including five classics, and on his death bed he wrote to Charlie saying how much he appreciated their friendship, "considering others gave me up." His headstone carried the epitaph: "It is not the race we ride, but 'tis the pace we go."

Over the next three years Charlie ticked along, clocking up an average of 50 wins a year, winning several of the top races for some of the most prominent owners.

In 1879, on Captain Machell's Mandarin, he secured the Royal Hunt Cup, beating a field of 30. He was also victorious in the Stewards Cup at Goodwood, on the notoriously difficult Peter; the Ascot Plate on Sir John Astley's Drumhead, and the Chesterfield Stakes on the rising Bend Or (who went on to win the Derby). By the end of the 1879 season, for the first time, Fred Archer, who had stood unrivalled as champion jockey since 1874, found Charlie snapping at his heels with 89 wins.

As their rivalry grew, both jockeys went to enormous efforts to clock up winners. The *Sydney Sportsman* ran an article titled 'A Doubtful Punishment' detailing how Charlie had been booked to ride at the November meeting in Manchester in 1879. He had no winners but found himself in front of the stewards with Archer and Jim Snowden for disobedience at the start. The other two escaped with a severe reprimand, but Charlie found himself suspended for the remainder of the meeting. He immediately set off for Kempton Park in London. His first mount proved successful and during the succeeding afternoons he had several winners. "Naturally, the reigning powers regarded Charlie's enforced withdrawal from Manchester as a punishment, but it must have afterwards dawned upon them as being somewhat ineffectual."[40]

Charlie was also establishing a reputation for being able to recognise and seize an opportunity more quickly than his rivals. Alexander Scott, in *Turf Memories of Sixty Years*, published in 1924, was a great admirer. "After Archer, Fordham and Constable, I think Charlie Wood was the next best judge of a horse and a handicap I ever knew. In addition, he was a superb horseman in the old style of riding." In the late 1870s the author heard a great compliment paid to Charlie's abilities as a jockey by the famous bookmaker, Dick Dunn. Standing up in Tattersalls Ring at Lewes races the bookie shouted that he was not laying horses for the race, which had 16 runners: "You can have 5-4 against Archer, and 5-4 against Wood, and any price you like against the other jockeys."

The early 1880s were to be Charlie and Archer's golden years. Charlie was 25 as the decade started and reaching his prime. Archer was 23 and had been champion jockey for seven years. Charlie was the established jockey for Joseph Dawson, while Archer was the stable jockey for Mathew Dawson, riding the magnificent horses of Lord Falmouth as his primary owner.

---

[40] Sydney Sportsman, December 23rd, 1903

In late 1880, however, tragedy struck when Joseph Dawson died from diabetes-related complications. Charlie lost the stability of his leadership and establishment as well as the trainer's unswerving support for his protégé. There was a relatively seamless transition as Harriet, Joseph's widow, took on her husband's headman, Richard Sherrard, to run the stables. Sir George Chetwynd was also established at Bedford Lodge and Chetwynd proudly proclaimed Charlie to be "my jockey."

It was about this time that Sir Francis Lawley first got to know Charlie.

"Between the commencement of 1880 and the middle of 1881, I had many opportunities of conversing with Wood while riding by his side on Newmarket Heath, of forming my own estimation of his character, and of appreciating his general intelligence, courage and skill in the saddle. I saw in him none of that 'disingenuousness of countenance... that failing to meet your eye firmly', often attributed to him by his enemies, and with a pretty long acquaintance with jockeys to guide me, I do not hesitate to say I believe Wood in 1880 to have been a creditable specimen of his class."[41]

Charlie, Chetwynd and Sherrard soon moved away and when Charlie built his own stables in 1884 opposite the gallops on Newmarket Heath, which he called Chetwynd House, Sherrard rented the yard.

They were full of optimism for the future. In one year Sherrard trained 135 winners, and Charlie rode 120 of them.[42]

---

[41] The Bench and the Jockey Club, Sir Francis Lawley, 1889
[42] Coventry Evening Telegraph, November 21st, 1935

But their successful joint venture would become the Jockey Club's main target before the decade was finished.

Sir George Chetwynd was a powerful personality who lived life on the edge and was obsessed with racing. He had become the 4th Baronet of Brocton Hall in 1869, following the death of his father. A tall, slight and distinguished looking man with the regulation moustache and sideburns, he was said to have considerable charm when he chose to exert it, along with a fiery temper. He owned racehorses before he was of age, running them under a pseudonym.

FAMOUS OWNERS.   No. 5.—SIR GEORGE CHETWYND, Bart.

Sir George Chetwynd
© Illustrated London News Ltd/Mary Evans

In 1870, he married the widowed Marchioness of Hastings. The Marchioness was famous in her own right for her elopement six years earlier, on the eve of her wedding. Then Lady Florence Paget, she was affianced to Henry Chaplin and drove with him to Swan and Edgar's in London to buy part of her trousseau. But she was passionately attached to the wild Marquess of Hastings and left the West End shop by a different door, meeting the marquess outside and eloping with him. Chaplin had his revenge three years later when he won the Derby with the rank outsider Hermit. The marquess, as was his habit, bet heavily on the race and lost over £100,000 [£11.6m], "Hermit fairly broke my heart. But I did not show it, did I?"[43] He was bankrupt and dead by the age of 26. Three years later, his widow married Chetwynd, after he promised not to lose his fortune racing. They went on to have a son and two daughters.

The baronet was the subject of many colourful stories and one related to the pickpockets who frequented most race meetings.

"When Sir George Chetwynd's tie-pin was stolen at Newmarket, he complained to the Earl of Lonsdale, knowing the 'Sporting Earl' enjoyed a nodding acquaintance with a selection of the rogues who frequented the racecourse. In time the pin was returned – by an individual dressed up as a vicar – at the cost of £25 to Sir George. Even worse, as he was leaving the races, Sir George was accosted by a scruffy looking boy who demanded to know how much he had paid for the pin's return. On hearing the sum the scruffy urchin exclaimed with disgust "Blimey! Twenty-five nicker. 'E only gave me ten bob when I stole the bloody thing.'"[44]

---

[43] Kings of the Turf, Thormanby, (William Dixon), 1898
[44] The Fast Set, George Plumptre, 1985

In 1871, at the age of 22, Chetwynd was elected as a member of the Jockey Club, and for a spell was the Senior Steward. From the start he made no secret of the fact that he looked to make a living from racing, and some members of the club, notably Lord Durham, viewed that as demeaning. It was one of the triggers for Durham's later attack.

Whatever his fellow Jockey Club members thought, at his height Chetwynd was said to be earning £6,000 [£770,000] a year out of racing and just before the storm clouds started to gather, a profile appeared in the *Illustrated Sporting and Dramatic News* on July 2nd, 1887 projecting him as a beacon of probity.

> "Sir George Chetwynd has been a member of the Jockey Club ever since 1871, and for many years played a leading part in the deliberations of that body. He made an energetic and efficient steward of the club, and is well qualified to purge the turf of the corruptions to which, as an institution, she is peculiarly obnoxious."

After Joseph Dawson's death, Charlie and Chetwynd put their faith in the abilities of Richard 'Buck' Sherrard. A short man, with the fashionable full beard and moustache, he had learnt his trade from Joseph Dawson, and followed his approach to feeding, managing and training horses.

George Lambton, Lord Durham's brother, later said the trainer was a nice man who simply loved his horses and thought of nothing else. He never left them for a moment, was most particular about every little detail, and never bet. Lambton said he did not think he had ever "seen horses turned out looking so beautiful."

In the years before the Jockey Club started targeting his stables, Sherrard trained for Chetwynd and Ernest Benzon, a foolish young man who inherited a large fortune and became known as the "Jubilee Plunger" for his gambling addiction. He lost it all. General Owen Williams and Lord Lurgan also kept their horses there.

Richard Sherrard. Pall Mall Gazette

Chetwynd soon built up a good string of horses. Utilising the combined skills of his trainer and jockey, racing author Alexander Scott says he was always difficult to beat for the simple reason that each member of the trio was a master of his particular job. George Lambton agreed: "Good as Sherrard was in the stable and on the training ground, about the form of horses and racing he knew little."[45] But with Chetwynd and Charlie on hand that did not matter, "For what these two did not know was not worth knowing." It was the perfect marriage of skills.

---

[45] Men and Horses I have Known, George Lambton, 1924

SHERRARD'S STABLES, CHETWYND HOUSE, NEWMARKET.

Sherrard's stables, Chetwynd House, Newmarket. Pall Mall Gazette

In 1881 Archer had 220 wins to Charlie's 153. In 1882 Archer again kept a clear lead with 220 to Charlie's 182. Archer was well aware of the rival on his heels, whom he said he respected for his wonderful judgement of pace and his ability to always put himself into a good position in a race.

As the 1881 season progressed, the *London Evening Standard* commented that Charlie had established himself as:

"An excellent horseman, who goes to scale at 7st 8lb, and who at the time of writing stands second to Archer in the list of winning jockeys. Charles Wood has ridden 351 races, and has won just ninety-nine. These figures are in themselves eloquent, and proclaim Wood a master of his art; for a stable-boy may, by good luck and a flash of inspiration, win a Derby, but to maintain an average means skilful horsemanship. In spite of his light weight, Wood displays much power in the saddle, and is the trusted rider for an astute coterie."[46]

There was still one prize that had eluded Charlie. On Derby day the country pretty much ground to halt as everyone focused on the big race and riding the winner put the "guinea stamp" on a jockey's career.

On the morning of May 24th, 1883, the House of Commons voted to close for the day so its members could attend Epsom that afternoon. Charlie was booked to ride St Blaise, trained by leading trainer John Porter at Kingsclere. St Blaise was given no chance against Lord Falmouth's Galliard, ridden by Fred Archer. Archer's brother, Charles, trained another runner in the race, Highland Chief.

The finish was charged with intense excitement:

"As they near the Grand Stand, and one horse creeps out from the ruck, there goes up the cry which no one who has been to Epsom on Derby day will ever forget – "Galliard wins" then "Highland Chief wins" and last of all there is a great burst of triumph as St Blaise springs to the front and passes the judge, the winner by a bare neck."[47]

It was so tight that, as the horses galloped past the post, even Charlie was not sure he had won and told the mounted police who had come to escort him that they had the wrong horse. St Blaise's joint owner Sir Frederick Johnson was also convinced Highland Chief had won, exclaiming: "By God, we're done."

[46] London Evening Standard, September 24th, 1881
[47] The Yorkshire Pocket Library No 9, The Life of Charles Wood, The Favourite Jockey

Then St Blaise's number went up. In his memoir, *Men, Women and Things*, the Duke of Portland remembered the victory well.

"From the Jockey Club stand we all thought [Lord Ellesmere's] Highland Chief had won, and Ellesmere walked down the steps to lead the horse in. As he did so St Blaise's number appeared on the winning frame, instead of that of his own horse. I never saw anyone show more self-control under such very trying and disappointing circumstances. He did not turn a hair, but simply turned round and walked up again."

Charlie had made his name. "The best race I rode was when I won the Derby on St Blaise in 1883. I beat Fred Webb and Fred Archer by a neck and half a length."[48]

The *New Zealand Mail* later said that the way he brought St. Blaise round Tattenham Corner, hugging the rails so closely that he could have put his leg outside them: "Was marvellous, and not even Fred Archer, famed as he was for drawing the corners fine, ever came within such a hair's breadth of a tremendous cropper."[49]

In his memoir, *Racecourse and Covert Side*, Alfred Edward Watson applauded the jockey. "Wood has courage and judgement. The former won him the Derby on St Blaise, the dash round the rails enabling him to get a forward place he never lost."

Charlie later said his boot grazed the rail, but the risky move gave him a six or seven lengths' advantage, just enough to win the race as Highland Chief came at a tremendous pace at the finish.

The *Licensed Victuallers' Gazette*, the newspaper Charlie would later take to court, was fulsome in its praise and did not begrudge

---

[48] Coventry Evening Telegraph, November 21st, 1935
[49] New Zealand Mail, March 18th, 1897

him the sums he earned with two notable wins. "One word more of congratulation to Charlie Wood who has now ridden his first Derby winner. He was a long time learning to be a really good jockey but has deservedly earned that rank. This season he has been in great form, and his earnings over Primrose II and St Blaise, will constitute a pretty little sum picked up in less than a week."[50]

The victory also brought Charlie to the attention of royalty. The *Hartford Courant* published a report in the United States that would never have made it into the English papers. It focused on the unbridled joy of the Prince of Wales after St Blaise's victory. The Prince was rumoured to have a connection with St Blaise and had certainly placed a large bet on the big slashing chestnut with a white blaze and three white feet.

The rumour was fuelled by the fact that he had watched the horse in a trial before the Derby, sitting on John Porter's trusty grey cob and shaking hands with Charlie and the trainer, inviting the latter to lunch at the Derby. After the victory, the paper commented:

"As for the prince himself, I never saw him so transported. I don't think I should be thought impolite if I said he was a heavyweight. Scribes less accustomed to English reticence in writing of royalty would say England's next King is as fat as a cask of butter. But all the same the portly personage of whom I speak is not given to rapid exercises or feats of agility. If, however, you had seen the Prince of Wales dance across the unsaddling enclosure, in which stands the royal boxes, and noticed how effusively he wrung the little red fist of honest John Porter of Kingsclere,... no one could

---

[50] Licensed Victuallers' Gazette, May 26th, 1883

have doubted that a very large stake has fallen to the
'*Ich dien*' motto."[51]

At one point it looked as if the Prince was on the point of
kissing Charlie: "But fortunately for the national reputation for
insouciance this did not happen." To the reporter's amusement
there was a lot of handshaking, with everybody congratulating
everyone else:

> "And the very considerable section of the House of
> Lords present solemnly kowtowed to each other and to
> the prince, like a set of the bald headed china figures
> which wag their heads mechanically on the slightest
> movement been given them."

In an interview in 1935, Charlie revealed how his relationship
with the Prince grew. "I met all the famous figures of those days,
... I remember an owner bringing the Prince of Wales (later
King Edward VII) to see me one day, and the Prince said, 'What
will win this race, Wood?' I said, 'Paradox; it is worth a bet, your
Royal Highness.' Well, Paradox won, and after that I put his
Royal Highness on plenty of winners. He always came or sent
someone to me for my opinion."[52]

The race had a very different outcome for Fred Archer, riding
the favourite Galliard. Archer was at the height of his popularity,
riding for one of the leading owners – Lord Falmouth – who was
said to be incorruptible and never bet. When Archer finished a
poor third, the rumour that he had pulled the favourite in favour
of his brother's horse, Highland Chief, took hold. Lord Falmouth
was said to be dissatisfied with the way Archer rode. In February

[51] Hartford Courant, June 13th, 1883
[52] Coventry Evening Telegraph, November 21st, 1935

the following year Falmouth disposed of his bloodstock and the rumour persisted that it was due to Galliard's failure in the Derby.

At the close of the 1883 season Charlie had won 186 races. He rode almost as many races as Fred Archer – 622 in all – but was still lagging some distance behind Archer, who led the rankings with 232 wins.

The *Yorkshire Pocket Library* published a history of his career to date, *The Life of Charles Wood, The Favourite Jockey.* "Charles Wood, one of the most talented riders of the Nineteenth Century, served his apprenticeship as jockey to the late Joseph Dawson… From small beginnings he has attained at a bound his present popularity."

Family owned trophy presented to Charles Wood by Mr Mackenzie
for winning the Chatsworth Plate in 1884

1884 saw the start of some substantive changes in the rules of racing, in particular the introduction of a ban on jockeys owning horses. As a result, in January the *Yorkshire Herald* reported that Charlie Wood had sold all of his horses to Sir George Chetywnd.

The nature of these transactions would form a major part of Charlie and Chetwynd's troubles four years later.

The Derby that year saw Charlie mounted on John Hammond's St Gatien, a big, elegant bay with a white blaze and three white socks. The horse was not well favoured, starting with long odds of 100 to 8, although a report at the time noted:

> "Wood rode [St Gatien] and that, in itself, was enough to make many people go 'nap' on the colt. When he stripped down in the paddock, with a hard, wear and tear, business-like appearance, he also attracted the late money. He was not fashionably bred, but was deep bodied, well ribbed up, with great powerful quarters and thighs, and good hocks... He stands over a lot of ground, too, and that he is of fine manners and temper is shown in the statement that during the preliminaries he never turned a hair; indeed, his coolness throughout the ordeal was the conspicuous feature."[53]

A quarter of a mile into the race, St Gatien showed in front, but Charlie held him back and let the outsider Borneo take up the running. Queen Adelaide was the favourite and in all probability the filly (mares could run in the Derby in those days) would have won but for being shut out and having to come a long way round.

> "It seemed all over. The yells went up
> 'Harvester wins! wins in a canter!'
> But the yielded inch of a tightened rein
> Has let up his face to the front again,
> And see, where Wood like a statue stands,
> High in his stirrup with downward hands.

---

[53] The Sportsman, May 29th, 1884

'St Gatien comes! St Gatien, for a pony!' is now the cry. The pair dash on neck and neck, closely followed by Queen Adelaide. It is all over. 'St Gatien! St Gatien!' is again the cry, as Harvester 'pecks' and Mr Hammond's colt takes the lead; but with a desperate effort Sam Loates pulls Sir John Willoughby's horse together, and riding him hard, shoots out and catches St Gatien on the post amidst the wildest and most deafening shouts it has ever been our lot to hear upon any racecourse."[54]

Charlie had ridden the second dead heat in the history of the Derby, and it was one of the most famous finishes he ever rode. "Harvester had beaten me at one time. He had as good as won but he pecked, and my horse got up again, and made a dead heat. If it had not been for that peck, Harvester would have won the Derby, sure enough. My horse was a bit sore, though, and the hard ground didn't suit him."

The race highlighted the huge sums that could be won or lost in a race in those days. St Gatien's owner, Hammond, was a controversial figure in racing. A former Newmarket stable boy who became too heavy to ride, he took to touting. He was blessed with keen eyes and sharp wits and quickly won a considerable sum of money. He soon became a professional backer and owner of a stud of racehorses. Despite his humble origins he was allowed to train his horses in the aristocratic Newmarket as he was said to have an irreproachable reputation, although he would later find his name dragged into the attempt to ruin Charlie.

Having seen St Gatien's performance in the trials before the race, he bet £45,000 [£5.8m] on the horse winning. He also put money on Harvester. That same year St Gatien went on to win

[54] Sporting Times, January 26th, 1889

the Cesarewitch, bringing in another £90,000 [£11.42m] for Hammond.

In 1885, Charlie was offered the ride on one of the all-time great racehorses, St Simon, owned by the Duke of Portland and trained by Mathew Dawson. Charlie initially got the ride because Fred Archer could not make the weight, and he rode St Simon in his four starts and four victories as a three year old.

St Simon, winner of the Goodwood Cup, engraving 1884
Artokolloro Quint Lox Limited/ Alamy Stock Photo

Mathew Dawson, who was said to have an infallible instinct about men and horses and could sense a rogue within a few minutes, was a strong supporter of Charlie. The Duke of Portland later stood up in court to defend Charlie's reputation. When the Duke wrote his memoir *Memories of Racing and Hunting* in the 1930s he dedicated it, with gratitude, to all those who had helped him through his racing career, including "Charles Wood, who rode St Simon when he won the Ascot Gold Cup."

The way the Duke acquired St Simon was a tale of how Mathew Dawson outwitted his own brother. John Dawson trained for St Simon's first owner, the Hungarian Prince Batthyany, who dropped dead at the races in early 1883. His death meant that all St Simon's entries into the classics were lost. The Prince's horses were all put up for sale, and Portland was particularly interested in a three-year-old called Fulmen. The Duke and Mathew Dawson went to see Fulmen and stopped to take a look at the two-year-old St Simon, by the great stallion Galopin, in the next box.

> "We noticed that its hock had been dressed with some white substance. I asked Mat if he thought it had a curb! He passed his hand over the place and said he did not think there was anything the matter in the least; adding that the stuff smelt more like paint than blister."[55]

Dawson suspected that his brother was trying to put off potential buyers and advised the Duke to bid for him the next day. Portland bought the horse for £1,600 guineas. Mathew Dawson said the horse went on to be the best he had ever trained and possibly the best that ever ran on the turf. When St Simon died, Portland had the horse's hide displayed at his stately home, Welbeck. His skeleton is stored at the Natural History Museum in London.

St Simon was unstoppable in every sense. In training as a two-year-old, Fred Archer made the mistake of touching him with his spur and the horse shot off. They quickly disappeared from view. Trainer and owner galloped in hot pursuit, to find a shaken jockey on foot holding the horse, declaring he had never been so fast through the air before.

---

[55] The Life of Mathew Dawson, Edith Humphris, 1928

Charlie rode St Simon in the Ascot Cup in 1884, where the main rival was a horse called Tristan. He trailed a long way behind at the start, but by midway through the race he had levelled with the competition. The rest of the field then appeared to stand still as St Simon took off to win by 20 lengths. Charlie did not manage to pull him up until he had gone nearly a mile past the post.

In 1885 Charlie was asked by the *Illustrated Sporting and Dramatic News* whether the horse he rode to a dead heat in the Derby, St Gatien, was the best he ever rode. He paused to consider and replied: "I shouldn't like to say which of the two – St Simon or St Gatien. Both wonderfully good horses; I can't say which is the best. I never knew how fast St Simon could go. In that match with Tristan he flew at the finish, and Tristan's a speedy horse; but as soon as I asked St Simon to leave him, he set off – ." The paper says at this point words failed Charlie and he put out his hands with an expressive gesture, as if he had hold of St Simon's head and was going on to win. He told the *Coventry Evening Telegraph* in November 1935: "I have ridden some splendid horses, but in my opinion St Simon was the best of them all. I never knew how fast he could go, because he was never extended."

In 1886, Archer had another good season and his major win that year was his fifth Derby on the great Ormonde. Charlie came a close second on General Owen Williams and Robert Peck's The Bard. But Archer's health was clearly affecting his riding and worrying his colleagues, to the point that they felt the need to take the pressure off him over that year's championship. In an interview in 1935 with the *Evening Standard*, Charlie said:

"'I was runner-up to Fred Archer for the jockey championship seven times,' [he said]. 'Poor Fred. Unlike me, he had to waste hard, and it ruined his health. I could always ride at 7st 10lb without any trouble. I remember on one occasion Fred's valet came to me and said: 'Mr Wood, you know Mr Archer is ill, and he is worrying himself to death that you will beat him, and he cannot stand it.' I said: 'Give my compliments to Mr Archer, and tell him I won't beat him. I'll miss the meeting – and I did.'"

The *Evening Star* reported that Charlie could have beaten Archer to the championship that year. Instead, he tried to finish the season with exactly the same total of wins. "But luck went against him at Manchester on the winding-up afternoon, and he only scored a single victory instead of the four that seemed well within his grasp."[56]

It was all to no avail. As the 1886 season drew to a close, Archer went to extreme lengths to keep his weight down. In particular, he was desperate to ride St Mirin at 8st 7lb in the Cambridgeshire as, if he could win, the rumour was that he would have netted £50,000 [£6m] in bets. He came second. After riding at Brighton and Lewes he had to give up the rest of his engagements as a fever took hold. By November 7th, 1886 he was delirious. On the afternoon of the next day he diverted the attention of his sister, who had been left in temporary charge of him by the professional nurse. While her head was turned, he sprang out of bed, grabbed the revolver he kept in the room and before he could be prevented, put the barrel in his mouth and fired.[57]

Following Archer's untimely death, the *New Zealand Herald* visited Northampton races and interviewed Charlie, who had just ridden a winner.

---

[56] Evening Star, February 5th, 1887
[57] Kings of the Turf, Thormanby, (William Dixon), 1898

"After he dismounted and passed the scales correctly I spoke to him. He is about five feet two, with a robust, healthy appearance, inclined to be slightly bandy, and was wearing his yellow silk jacket and cardinal cap... He said: 'I never waste except for an exceptional mount. Even then my wasting seldom exceeds three or four pounds, which makes me feel very weak' adding, 'Try yourself to do without your ordinary food, taking instead Turkish baths and seidlitz powders [a laxative with severe side effects] for a week, and you will also feel bad, I can tell you.'"

In the Kings of the Turf, William Dixon was clear that fasting had played its part:

"There can be no doubt that Fred Archer was never the same man after the death of his wife, and there can be just as little doubt that he fatally weakened his system by his drastic methods of reducing his weight... Archer suffered greatly from the process, which always made him feverish and irritable. But he would take no warning nor advice on the subject, though it was sheer madness to suppose that a man who even as a boy could not ride under six stone... could with impunity get himself down to 8st 7lbs at the age of thirty. At the same time it adds greatly to the brilliancy of Archer's career that he should have so completely outdistanced all rivals in the number of his winning mounts when his weight prevented him from riding lightly handicapped horses."[58]

---

[58] Kings of the Turf, Thormanby, (William Dixon), 1898

As the decade drew on, Archer and Charlie's obvious wealth, and the tales of big bets and large presents from owners, had started to cause concern among some Jockey Club members. In Archer's last year, he and Charlie found themselves unsuccessfully challenging income tax assessments for earnings in excess of £10,000 [£1.25m] a year. In the early part of the 1880s they had both built themselves palatial establishments in Newmarket. Before his marriage in 1882, Archer built Falmouth Lodge for the sum of £20,000 [£2.5m], where he intended to train when his riding days were finished.

Charlie soon followed suit. A journalist from the *Sporting Life* was walking through Newmarket in September 1884, when he met: "One of our leading handicappers and clerks of the course. 'I have been making inquiries,' said he, pointing to stately massive brick buildings, 'whose place that is, and I find it is Charlie Wood's, the jockey, who has spent about £7,000 [£850,000] for a training establishment.'" The journalist learnt that Richard Sherrard would soon be taking up residence as manager, and Charlie Wood was having Sir John Astley's house and the one next to it knocked into one for his private use.

> "I looked over the buildings – not yet, of course, in complete order... The brickwork is the best I ever saw in my life... There are thirty-two boxes, and a couple of six stall stables, accommodation thus being provided for 44 horses. The yard occupies a grand space, so that in winter on the straw track there is ample room for exercise, while the proximity to the Heath simply means popping out of the yard gates and onto the grass."[59]

---

[59] Sporting Life, September 25th, 1884

Charlie's new yard had spacious and lofty boxes, and long zinc lined mangers. He had his initials cast on a plaque with the year the yard was completed, which is still there today. *The Badminton Library*, in its edition on racing in 1887, included the plans and drawings of the yard. It concluded that they were "exceptionally well arranged." The yard is still in use, now called Machell Place.

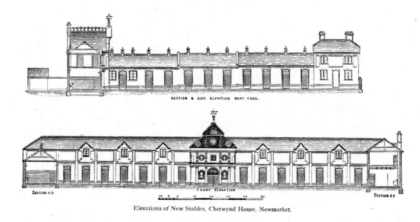

Elevations of New Stables, Chetwynd House, Newmarket.

Chetwynd Stables
The Badminton Library

Charlie moved his family to live in Lowther House on Newmarket High Street and started investing in property in the town, including two pubs – the Greyhound and the Black Horse Inn. He also built a stud farm in the outskirts. It all seemed very ostentatious for a jockey earning the regulation £5 a win, and he soon earned the nickname Lord Newmarket.

In 1887, he became champion jockey. He had won over 150 races and was the nation's favourite jockey. At the age of 35, he was set to enjoy many years at the top of his profession. He had no ride in the Derby that year, but had won the Oaks and the 1,000 Guineas on the Duke of Beaufort's Reve d'Or.

C. WOOD, WHO WILL RIDE GALTEE MORE.

CHAPTER NINE

Derby Day, 1897

Sam Darlings hands him his cap

Charlie walks into the weighing in room, dressed in John Gubbins' silks – a crimson cap and violet shirt with crimson buttons – carrying Galtee More's saddle.

THE DERBY: THE WEIGHING ROOM. EPSOM.

The Derby Weighing Room – Owners and Trainers check on their jockeys, 1893
Lordprice Collection / Alamy Stock Photo

The weighing room at Epsom sees the first convergence of jockeys and officials and it is a tense meeting between Charlie and his old enemies, the top hatted members of the Jockey Club. He is surrounded by some of the leading jockeys of the day, Jack Watts, Morny Cannon, Otto Madden and Sam Oates.

The last time he had sat in this room before a Derby was in 1886. Fred Archer had won that day on the Duke of Portland's Ormonde, with Charlie a close second on The Bard. He had been secure in his place in that world; along with Archer he had been one of the most popular jockeys in the country, with friends and supporters in the highest echelons of society.

Today, as he sits once more on the huge bronze balance scales, he knows just how naive he had once been. He had thought that his success would protect him from his enemies. He had no inkling how that success would be twisted into a weapon that his enemies would use to try to destroy him.

Charlie had kept his weight below eight stone all through his exile by riding and hunting with his wife Ellen, and this is now paying dividends as the officials take off some weights to find the right balance.

His walk from the weighing room to the paddock is almost as fraught as Galtee More's, as he has to struggle through the crowds blocking his way, all eager to see Charlie at his first Derby since his return to the saddle.

CHAPTER TEN

On Betting

My word, jockeys did bet in those days, dear readers

The 1880s proved a tumultuous decade for racing. The sport was the national obsession and betting was widespread. Huge sums could be won and anyone could bet. At the start of the decade that included jockeys.

Before the 1897 Derby there had been an attempt to ban all betting, but on the day the bookies were out in force.

"No Betting Allowed"
The Illustrated Sporting and Dramatic News, 1897
© Illustrated London News Ltd/Mary Evans

The earliest recorded races were match races between two or three horses, and the betting was between the owners and their connections – a gentleman's wager, winner takes all. By the mid 18th century there was more public racing with larger numbers of horses and gambling was on the rise. Race meetings were attracting large and potentially disorderly crowds and, in particular, they attracted working-class people, inducing them to 'miss work and become idle'.

The Jockey Club was founded in 1751 to regulate the growing sport, and in 1789 Tattersalls was created to regulate betting. As the 19th century arrived bookmakers started to emerge and betting became more widespread, offering predetermined odds on races.

With a growing middle class through the 19th century, gambling on horse racing took off and: "The social conflict of the time, in terms of social hierarchy due to birth and social hierarchy due to wealth was to be fought in part through gambling."[60]

In 1845 the Gaming Act barred all betting except on the racecourse. The middle classes were demanding its complete abolition to protect the working classes. The upper classes, although not wanting gambling abolished: "Wanted the debasing of their noble pursuits by the working classes stopped."[60]

In the late 1870s the Jockey Club tried to ban jockeys from betting, a move strongly resisted by the jockeys. They made further attempts through the 1880s, which were largely ignored.

The relationship between jockeys, trainers and owners also underwent a radical change as the decade wore on, as the wealth

[60] May 2000 KPMG report for Business in Sport & Leisure, 'The Economic Value and Public Perceptions of Gambling in the UK', updated, Donoughue, GamblingConsultants.co.uk

and power started to filter away from the aristocracy into the hands of the trainers and jockeys.

In large part the aristocracy had only itself to blame. The membership of the Jockey Club came entirely from the upper classes. They elected themselves and jealously guarded their self-appointed role as the governing body of racing.

The Jockey Club, Newmarket. Drawn by F. G. Kitton.

Mary Evans Picture Library

Many of the members were making and losing fortunes betting and they voted down any attempt to rein in their practices. When Robert Black wrote *The Jockey Club and its Founders* in 1891 he heavily criticised its failure to curb the continued explosion in betting and the corrupt practices that inevitably followed.

As Black points out, the Jockey Club did not even have clean hands on the issue of stopping horses from winning races, as it had refused to ban the pernicious 'declaration to win'. A declaration about the intended outcome of a race the gentleman kept between themselves. In 1880 the respected trainer William Day, in his book *Racehorse in Training*, had no difficulty with the 'declaration to win' saying it was a disgraceful exhibition when a jockey won in defiance of an order to pull his horse when a declaration has been made. In his opinion the offending jockey should be heavily fined and suspended.

As Black noted, if the Jockey Club sanctioned having: "One or two horses pulled for the sake of winning not a race, be it observed, but the money you have betted on a race," it was no wonder that people could not see why you, "may not have a single horse pulled for the same commercially legitimate object."

As betting increased among the middle and lower classes, Black pointed out that the large amounts of money the members of the Jockey Club were winning in those days came partly from the pockets of members of the Jockey Club and gentlemen of their own class, but increasingly it also came from: "The perennial stream of the savings, the stealings, or the superfluities of the backing millions."

A nice thing, says Black, that a member of the Jockey Club, a Royal Prince, or a Duke, or a Marquess, or an Earl, or a mere Baronet: "Should win, if he do win, the money of his own tradesman or valet."[61]

While the members of the Jockey Club were busy winning and losing millions in bets, their servants, the jockeys, were expected to be content with earning a wage and the fee for riding a race, set at £5 for a win, supplemented by payments for riding trials.

As the 1880s began, the Jockey Club started to focus its attention on the jockeys, an increasing number of whom not only bet – and bet to an extravagant extent – but were owners or part owners of racehorses. New rules brought in the licensing of jockeys, a ban on their owning horses and some attempted limitations on their betting.

---

[61] The Jockey Club and its Founders, Robert Black, 1891

Robert Black questioned how, if the Jockey Club did not reform itself, the new rules could be expected to have any real impact: "So long as jockeys are human, with eyes to see the example set them by their employers, with ears to hear the suggestions of the tempter."

As the decade drew on, the relationship between jockeys and owners also began to change as the owners started to treat as equal the men who could deliver lucrative victories. The best jockeys, especially Fred Archer and Charlie, started to earn significant additional income through retainers, as owners wanted to secure first, second or even third call on their services.

On top of that, the presents they began to receive for a win started to worry some members of the Jockey Club. A gift of £1,000 [£130,000] became common for winning a big race.

The trainers were well aware of the impact such presents could have on a jockey. In 1874 Mathew Dawson put Fred Archer up on Tomahawk in the Lincolnshire Handicap, the first big race of the flat racing season. The horse romped home and the owner insisted on presenting the young jockey with £50 to the annoyance of the trainer. "This is the best boy I've ever had, and I'm not going to have his head turned," Dawson fumed. It was too late.

Able jockeys could earn upwards of £5,000 a year from fees and presents alone. If they added in some horse-dealing, betting and the occasional sale of information, it was quite possible to earn double that. At their height, Archer and Charlie earned well in excess of £10,000 [£1.2m] a year.

The amounts some jockeys bet on their own account became legendary. Alexander Scott wrote of a race at Windsor where he overheard Archer asking for a bet to be placed on a horse ridden by Charlie.

"The Windsor course has been productive of many surprises. I remember a hot favourite ridden by Fred Archer being beaten there, losing many people a lot of money. It did not cost the great Fred anything, though; on the contrary, he picked up a nice sum of £1,200 [£151,000] by his good judgement. In this same race was a horse called Cohort, owned by General Owen Williams, and ridden by Charlie Wood, Archer's great rival. When Fred was preparing to leave the paddock to canter down to the starting-post, I happened to be close to him. Fred bent down to his mount's neck and said to the man who saddled the horse: "Tell Arthur (Mr Arthur Cooper, his commissioner) to put me £200 on Cohort."[62]

Scott says Archer had been having a good look at Charlie's mount, and had made up his mind Charlie would beat him. Dashing into the ring, Scott got 6 to 1 on Cohort.

Archer was beaten by a neck, and Scott saw Cooper and asked him what he actually put on Cohort for Archer. "'£1,200 to £200' he replied, in astonishment at my knowing anything about it. 'It's quite all right, Arthur,' I assured him, 'I heard Fred tell the stableman what you were to do.'"

Scott concluded, "My word, jockeys *did bet* in those days, dear readers, not in paltry fivers or tenners, as you have seen."[63]

The *Gloucester Citizen* in July 1935, when reviewing the history of the Stewards Cup, told how in that race, in 1883, Fred Archer was riding a fast mare, Gehiemniss, but was beaten by a head.

---

[62] Turf Memories of Sixty Years, Alexander Scott, 1924
[63] Turf Memories of Sixty Years, Alexander Scott, 1924

"The winner was Hornpipe ridden by his famous rival, Charles Wood. Archer betted heavily at times. He stood to win a small fortune on the mare who the previous year had won the Oaks and had finished second in the St Leger. 'Having so much money at stake flurried Fred,' Wood said. 'He made too much use of Gehiemniss, considering the weight she had to carry. I just beat him in the very last stride.'"[64]

Charlie also regularly advised several of his owners on their betting, including members of the Jockey Club.

"There was some heavy gambling in those days. General Owen Williams. one of Sherrard's patrons, for whom I rode, was a real gambler. He would ask me how much to have on, and if I said £300 he would probably double or treble it. I had always to be careful in mentioning a figure. I remember the old Duchess of Montrose calling me into her bedroom one morning. She was in bed, and said, 'I have lost £700 this weekend, and you have got to get it back for me.' Well. I put her on a 6 to 1 winner, on which she had £500. She was a very wealthy woman, but she hated to lose even a 'tenner.'"[65]

Inevitably, there were rampant accusations of race fixing. The St Leger in 1881 shows just how vicious they could become, even against those with the impeccable reputations of Matthew Dawson and Lord Falmouth, and how the Jockey Club usually chose to ignore them.

---

[64] Gloucester Citizen, July 26th, 1935
[65] Coventry Evening Telegraph, November 21st, 1935

Dutch Oven, ridden by Archer, was a favourite for the St Leger until the horse was well beaten in an earlier race. It then won the big race and a section of backers clung to the idea that both races had been fixed by the horse's connections.

"After her victory Matthew Dawson was the recipient of some extraordinary letters, accusing him of every crime under the sun. Lord Falmouth also being favoured with like condemnatory epistles. Nor did Archer himself escape the fiery and perhaps undeserved attacks of anonymous correspondents."[66]

In 1884, Fred Archer was encouraged to sue the *Morning Post* for libel over its comments on his riding of Energy in the Portland Plate. The paper said in so many words that Archer backed a horse called Leeds, the winner, and in order to assure its victory, pulled his own mount, Energy. Lord Falmouth told Archer that he ought not to let such an insinuation pass and that it was his duty to indict the writer for libel. The paper backed down immediately.

With popular jockeys earning riding fees of £5 or less but starting to become obviously wealthy, rumours of betting and race fixing became commonplace There were persistent claims that Archer and Charlie were linked to a group of jockeys who fixed races between them. Sir George Chetwynd, during the time he was a Jockey Club Steward in the mid 1880s, heard that a group of jockeys were fixing races, including Archer and Charlie. He was certain a jockey ring did not exist but called the other Jockey Club Stewards' attention to the rumours. Nat Gould, the famous author and a contemporary jockey to Archer and Charlie, dismissed the rumours of a ring.

---

[66] Ashgill. The life and times of John Osborne, John Radcliffe, 1900

"Wood and Archer were once supposed to be the head of a jockey ring. I do not believe it for one moment. Charles Wood is alive and, I am glad to say well, and as good a jockey as one would ever wish to see he was in those days. He can speak for himself, and I am sure would bear me out when I say that neither he nor Fred Archer ever had anything to do with a jockey ring if there was one... The public – I mean the public who back horses – are not altogether fools and they would not have stuck to Archer as they did if they were not perfectly certain that he rode to win.

It is ridiculous to suppose for a moment that jockeys at the head of their profession would do such a thing. Probably there were jockeys who backed Archer and Charlie Woods' mounts, because they were perfectly certain they would beat their own... The idea of leading jockeys pulling horses on their own account is laughable."[67]

Archer's betting would, however, contribute to his downfall as he became increasingly worried about money. One report claimed he gradually received fewer presents from owners, as they assumed he had a big bet on for himself.

Towards the end of his last season in 1886, it was said that he had put a fortune on his mount, St Mirin, in the Cambridgeshire as he was £30,000 [£3.8m] down on his betting through the season. He got good odds as it was not the favourite and the rumour was that he would have netted £50,000 [£6m] with a win. He starved himself to get down from over 9st to 8st 7lb in order to make the weight but was beaten by Carlton. The defeat may have contributed to his suicide later that year.

---

[67] The Life of Mathew Dawson, Edith Humphris, 1928

By 1887, the press speculation about races being fixed showed no sign of abating and Lord Durham, a Jockey Club steward known for his reforming zeal, decided to take the issue head on. He would soon have Charlie, Richard Sherrard and Chetwynd in his sights but his first high profile and successful stroke was against a marquess.

Durham was the steward at York races in 1887 when he saw the Marquess of Ailesbury's horse, Everrett, race. His attention was caught by the fact that the horse was doing its best to win in spite of the most strenuous exertions of its rider to pull it back. It was so blatant that Durham reported the incident to the Jockey Club, which started an investigation. The jockey, Teddy Martin, confessed and turned Queen's evidence, and it became clear that he regularly got orders to lose races.

Ailesbury, "A young nobleman who had had to leave Eton because he refused to be flogged,"[68] had further damaged his social position by marrying a music hall singer known as Dollie Tester. Ailesbury was found to have given clear instructions for the horse to lose, apparently to spite someone who had a lot of money on Everrett.

The Jockey Club banned Ailesbury and warned him off Newmarket Heath. That it had the power to expel a marquess caused a sensation. A hereditary peer, he sat in the House of Lords and the press enjoyed pointing out that a man could be too corrupt to race and yet good enough to make laws for the Empire.

His success against a marquess gave Durham a taste for the work and as the 1887 season drew to a close, it quickly became apparent that the death of Fred Archer had left Charlie exposed to powerful enemies within the Jockey Club.

---

[68] The Gay Victorians, Ralph Nevill, 1930

CHAPTER ELEVEN

Derby Day, 1897

The paddock resembles a bear pit

The public and horses first meet in the big open area bounded by hedges known as the paddock. A large crowd is waiting, eager to see the horses and jockeys at close hand.

GALTEE MORE IN THE PADDOCK BEFORE SADDLING.

"Galtee More in the paddock before saddling"
The Illustrated Sporting and Dramatic News
© Illustrated London News Ltd/Mary Evans

As Galtee More's groom, Harry, walks him round behind his stable companion Glenmorgan, he is followed by over 500 people, including a proud Mr F Platt, the owner of Galtee More's sire, Kendal. Everyone agrees that the big bay colt towers over the field with his good looks, light movement and faultless shaping.

He stands out as the gentleman of the party and looks as muscular and hard as a prize fighter. With his "resolute eye" he looks over the crowd as if scorning defeat. The way he lashes out when Sam Darling tightens his girth is taken as showing he is as fit as a fiddle.

The Sketch puts its faith in Charlie and his mount:

> "The Derby looks a gift for Galtee More... It is a feather in the cap of Wood to get the mount of such a smasher, and I am glad to notice that the popular jockey retains the art of properly handling young horses. Wood may not be quite so quick out of the slips as he was 10 years ago, but he rides with the same perfect judgement as of yore, and he is a bad one to beat in a tight finish."

It may look a gift. But in the paddock there are 10 other groups of breeders, owners, trainers and jockeys also hoping this is going to be their day.

As the crowds mingle with the horses and inspect their favourites, a journalist from the *Sporting Times* is assessing the rest of the field in detail. Galtee More's main opposition is Lord Rosebery's Velasquez, ridden by Jack Watts in Rosebery's famous primrose and rose hoops and rose cap. He looks on his toes, fresh and well.

Prime Minister, a dark brown colt, is standing near the bottom of the paddock. He is a tough small horse of the long, low order. A cool, old-fashioned type. Under the hedge on the higher side of the paddock Monterey stands with his stable companion. He also has a well-trained look. Silver Fox does not attract much attention. He strips down a little lighter in his back ribs than followers of the Derby like. Eager is a muscular little horse but small, while Frisson shows more reach and scope, but loses followers because of his irritable behaviour.

The Prince of Wales's Oakdene, ridden by Otto Madden in the Prince's colours – purple body, with gold braid, scarlet sleeves, black cap, with gold fringe – is rather mean in size and quality but he has serviceable limbs and is in fine fettle. The last horse to come through is the clearly fit History. Ridden by Morny Cannon, the current champion jockey, he is one who could win if fortune favours him and his experienced jockey. Cannon has already been champion jockey five times, but as yet the coveted Derby win has eluded him.

"P.I.P." DERBY ANIMATOGRAPHE: CLEARING THE COURSE, AND ROUNDING TATTENHAM CORNER.

"Clearing the course and rounding Tattenham Corner"
The Penny Illustrated Paper

Once Mr Manning has the 11 jockeys weighed out and their numbers exhibited on the board, the jockeys are legged up onto their horses. The mounted police set about clearing the course of the immense mass of spectators roving all over it.

The order for the parade is given and John Gubbins' final instructions to Charlie are simple: "Don't be afraid of the corner and come home as soon as you can."

CHAPTER TWELVE

A Bolt from the Blue

When Charlie Wood almost pulled the head off

Charlie's life was turned upside down when, on November 25th, 1887 the *Licensed Victualler's Gazette and Hotel Courier* asked: "How about the running of Success at Lewes and Alexander Park, when Charlie Wood almost pulled the head off on each occasion?"

It was a shocking accusation. The paper baldly stated that Charlie was a cheat, that he had deliberately almost taken the head off the horse in his determination to slow it down and lose two races. If owners and trainers started to believe that of him, he would never ride in the important races again. Just as he had been crowned champion jockey, it could all be taken away from him.

Lord Durham was certainly in no mood to sympathise. He was enjoying his reputation as a reformer. His difficulty had been how to start his next assault. He overcame it by joining forces with the *Licensed Victuallers' Gazette*, which ran a regular column of racing gossip, and accepting an invitation to make the after dinner speech at the upcoming Gimcrack Club dinner in York.

The newspaper's accusation appeared three weeks after the race at Lewes, which had been on November 4th, 1887. Charlie had ridden the two-year-old gelding, Success, owned by General Owen Williams and trained in Newmarket by Martin Gurry. The horse had already raced twice that season, unplaced each time. Charlie picked up the ride at Lewes where he was third, half a length behind the second placed horse, which itself was beaten by a head. Eight days later they were unplaced at Alexandra

Park. The horse was sold that day (a transaction that was also later alleged to be suspect) and five days later it won the Highfield Selling Plate at Derby with a different jockey.

When the *Licensed Victualler's Gazette* accusation was published, Charlie showed it to the horse's owner General Williams, saying it was disgraceful. The general advised him it was in his own interests to ask for an inquiry. Anxious for the reputation of his jockey, he wrote to the Jockey Club asking for a full investigation, saying he had, and continued to have, the greatest confidence in Charlie.

John George Lambton, 3rd Earl of Durham
Chronicle / Alamy Stock Photo

Meanwhile, Durham and the Jockey Club started to close in on their other two targets, owner Sir George Chetwynd and trainer Richard Sherrard. Chetwynd received a letter from Messrs Weatherby, the Jockey Club's agents, on December 6th, 1887 asking him to account for the in-and-out running of Fullerton, trained by Richard Sherrard and often ridden by Charlie. Chetwynd immediately asked for a meeting where he could: "Prove to them in the most conclusive manner what calumnies the said comments are."

At the meeting Chetwynd produced his betting books, which clearly showed that he had lost money on the horse.

Despite that evidence, on the evening of December 13th, Durham delivered a devastating speech at the 121st annual meeting of the Ancient Fraternity of York Gimcracks at York's Harker Hotel, in a room dominated by the portrait of the magnificent grey racehorse, Gimcrack.

After the toast to "the Stewards and Patrons of York Races," Durham rose to respond:

> "I do so with great pleasure, because I am very fond of York races. I have also been a Steward this year, and had some unpleasant work to do... Though it really has nothing to do with the toast, I wish to say a few words on certain matters connected with the Turf, because there are few occasions on which we can put our opinions before the public."[69]

He then prepared the ground by stating that in future the Jockey Club would "withdraw the licence of any jockey who may be proved to have an interest in any racehorse or to have been engaged in any betting transactions," predicting that this rule, if enforced, would see a very different list of names of principal winning jockeys at the end of the next season. He warmed to his theme:

---

[69] The Bench and the Jockey Club, Sir Francis Lawley, 1889

"Surely the Stewards do not ignore what every racing man knows – that one or two jockeys bet in large sums, are virtual owners of horses which run in other person's names. It is notorious that one well known jockey does this. I have often been told, when I have asked who Mr So-and-So is, for whom the jockey rides, 'Oh that man's horse is really the jockey's property.' If I add to this, that it is a generally accepted fact that this jockey pulls horses in order that he may make money out of them, I think you will agree that this is a very serious evil to the Turf."

Durham turned his attention to those owners who employed such a jockey. "If we blame owners for putting up certain jockeys of ill-repute to win them races, what are we to say of owners who employ them to win money?"

If the Jockey Club was about to set off down this route, some of those in the room must have started to worry about how many great names would follow the Marquess of Ailesbury into shame before they, and more particularly Durham, were satisfied.

Durham declared that no owner of horses ought to put up any jockey suspected of, or known to be guilty of, pulling horses.

"Unfortunately I know many very honest and straightforward owners of horses who employ the services of a notorious jockey because he rides well and because they adopt the selfish principle that it is better to have him on their side than against them. I go further than this. Some owners employ him because they think he can 'square' some other jockeys in the race and thus ensure the victory for his mount if he has backed it. I consider such policy on the part of owners to be a direct encouragement to malpractice on the part of jockeys."

Durham then widened his attack.

"There is a well-known and what the sporting press calls a fashionable and aristocratic racing stables that has been conspicuous throughout the racing season for the constant and inexplicable in-and-out running of its horses... But the darkest part of the matter is this – that the owners and nominal owners of the horses to which I am alluding win large stakes when their horses are successful, but do not lose much when they are beaten."

This was taken to be a direct assault on Charlie, Chetwynd and the training yard at Chetwynd House, run by Richard Sherrard.

"If you wish to purify the Turf you must go to the fountain head ... I am certain that it is as much a matter of regret to all of [the members of the Jockey Club] as it is to me to see that some men equal to us in social position and in racing influence have failed to maintain the fair reputation of the turf."

The senior Jockey Club steward, James Lowther, rose in support and left those in the room in no doubt that the Jockey Club was saying that a fraud was being perpetuated on the sport. He implied they had clear evidence of a jockey ring, saying: "We found that jockeys not only betted, but, by means of cooperation, received through the agency of a third party, large sums." At which point Durham interjected, "On one horse." "Of course, on one horse. A good number of these jockeys unite their interests in one horse, and, of course, as many of them rode other horses, it could scarcely contribute to the welfare of the Turf." Lowther concluded: "If you want to stop thieving, you must get at the receivers."[70]

In the *Bench and the Jockey Club*, Sir Francis Lawley wrote of the evening:

"Never had a bolt that fell so suddenly from a blue and cloudless sky created more sensation than Durham's speech and Mr Lowther's apparent endorsement of it."

Initially the press did not take much notice of the speech, but within weeks it had led to a challenge to a duel and the launch of three suits for libel.

---

[70] The Bench and the Jockey Club, Sir Francis Lawley, 1889

CHAPTER THIRTEEN

Derby Day, 1897

To the start

THE PARADE.

"The Parade"
The Illustrated Sporting and Dramatic News, 1897
© Illustrated London News Ltd/Mary Evans

At three o'clock exactly, Charlie and Galtee More lead the rest of the field out onto the course for the parade. They trot down and canter back past the excited spectators gathered in the stands and lining the course with their carriages.

In the canter Velasquez, who looks ready to race and a handful for his jockey Jack Watts, comes up alongside Galtee More. It gives the crowd a chance to compare the way the lighter horse moves against the larger Galtee More, with his regular, machine like action and powerful hind legs.

The jockeys in their brightly coloured silks set off round to the start, with millions of pounds in bets riding with them.

Charlie knows he is on the horse the crowd has settled on as their favourite. He is expected to win, and he must win. But there are no 'dead certs' in racing. When he won his first Derby in 1883, the favourite came in third. And when he finished in a dead heat in the 1884 Derby, it was because the favourite pecked just before the finishing post.

If he comes even a close second, Darling and Gubbins will look like fools for choosing him as their jockey. He will be finished. The racing world will turn its back on him once more. Some will even whisper that he "pulled" the favourite. He will not get another chance.

Only a victory in this Derby will grant him the redemption he has sought for nine years. Knowing that makes this the most dangerous race he has ever ridden. He could so easily over ride Galtee More. He could misjudge the horse or the competition in the heat of the battle. Through his racing career he had come to rely on his ability to assess each stage of a race, timing his decisions to perfection. What if that ability has become clouded over the nine years of enforced idleness? Or by his advancing age? What if the fear of failure makes him hesitate?

Galtee More goes to the start the favourite. However, in the paddock, Velasquez's obvious fitness won over some of the racegoers seeing him for the first time and he starts attracting some of the late betting.

The crowds on the Hill rush from the booths to the rails to watch the horses pass. The rain clouds hang ominously, though not a drop falls.

CHAPTER FOURTEEN

Licence Lost

Banished

On December 15th, 1887, two days after the Gimcrack speech, James Lowther called Charlie into a hearing about Success, sitting with fellow stewards Lord Hastings and the Hon HW Fitzwilliam. He answered their questions and went to his winter home in Brighton for Christmas.

Charlie knew that they wanted him to show that he was taking William H Cox, the owner of the *Licensed Victuallers' Gazette* to court and had instructed his solicitor, the lawyer of choice in high society and the racing world, George Lewis, to issue criminal proceedings for libel. That had been done, but Charlie missed the date of the hearing at Bow Street Magistrates as the letter advising him of the date did not arrive until after he had left Newmarket for Brighton.

He then had a shock when he received a letter from George Lewis saying that he could no longer act for him as he was instructed by Lord Durham in the affair and the papers would be returned on payment of the bill.

Durham and the Jockey Club always strenuously denied that his speech had been drawn up by the Jockey Club and that Durham had been selected as the mouthpiece. The suspicion that there was also collusion between Durham and the *Licensed Victuallers' Gazette* grew once it became known that Durham had chosen the newspaper's legal team, including Charlie's original solicitors, and that the noble lord was going to pick up the costs.

On January 4th, 1888 Charlie received all of the correspondence back and needed to find a new lawyer. The Jockey Club was keeping up the pressure and on January 6th he received a letter from Edward Weatherby on their behalf asking whether he was going to bring a libel action, as their inquiry into the running of Success was not closed. Charlie replied, saying that he had not instructed a new solicitor as he wanted to wait until the return of Success's owner, General Owen Williams, who was in India and would not be back before Easter.

The Jockey Club stewards were in no mood to wait and on January 13th he was called back and closely questioned on the riding of Success.

One day later, after they took evidence from other witnesses, without him being allowed to be present or challenge the allegations made against him, Charlie learnt that he had lost his licence.

His 17-year career as a jockey was wiped out with this one announcement. The press reports said that the grounds included the suspicion that he owned some racehorses and that he had failed to satisfy the stewards about the running of Success during the 1887 season.

His persecutor in chief, the *Licensed Victuallers' Gazette*, applauded the move, saying opinions might differ over whether the sentence of banishment was inevitable, but it had: "No sympathy with those whiners who prate about over-severity. The Stewards clearly found that a strong warning was necessary, and no right-thinking person can blame them for carrying out what they felt to be their duty."[71]

The paper had no issue with the fact that no one other than the Jockey Club knew the basis of their decision, saying it was to be hoped that a time might come when they will deem it reasonable to restore to the suspended jockey the privileges he

---

[71] Licensed Victuallers' Gazette, January 20th, 1888

had until now enjoyed, but on this point: "The authorities must be the best judges as they alone know the exact particulars of the evidence on which they came to make the determination which has caused such talk."

However, Charlie had been subjected to a trial without representation or the right to hear the case against him. He had attended two meetings where he was examined with regard to his riding, but he was not present when any of the invited witnesses were examined by the Jockey Club.

The Duke of Beaufort was outraged and took up the cudgels on behalf of his favourite jockey. When the stewards refused Charlie's request to rehear his application for his licence Beaufort instructed his solicitors, Messrs Greenfield and Cracknell, to investigate. They wrote to the Jockey Club:

> *3, Lancaster-place, W.C, London, January 31, 1888.*
>   Sir,
>   The Duke of Beaufort has requested us to investigate the circumstances relating to the riding of Success upon which the Stewards of the Jockey Club have recently refused to grant to Charles Wood, the jockey, his annual licence to ride; and, as Wood was not present or represented when the witnesses were examined, upon whose testimony, we presume, the Stewards acted, we trust they will allow you to send on behalf of Wood (for whom we respectfully make the request), a copy of the notes of all the evidence taken at the inquiry.
> We are, Sir, your obedient servants,
>   (Signed) GREENFIELD and CRACKNELL

In reply Edward Weatherby, on behalf of the Jockey Club, simply refused the request.

The *Pall Mall Gazette* was unsettled by the way the Jockey Club approached its business, noting: "It is curious to see how utterly the Jockey Club is at variance with all the ideas which are generally accepted nowadays as to the proper constitution of governing authority. It is a close corporation which is in no sense whatever representative."

Its members, it said, were added from time to time but solely by co-option.

"They select whom they please, and reject whom they please: the only unwritten law which seems to govern their otherwise unlimited range of selection is that Masters of the Buckhounds are always added to the Club, even if those members of the Royal household happen to be as innocent of the ownership of racehorses as Adam himself... It is doubtful whether any other body could have struck down, as it has done within the last few weeks without the slightest effort, the jockey who stood at the very head of his profession, and who is besides a man of immense wealth. The Stewards of the club, however, merely refused Wood his licence, and henceforth the racecourses of England are forbidden ground to the first horseman in the country... Powers so vast, however, entail a commensurate responsibility, and the fact that the Jockey Club can do as it pleases is the strongest of reasons why it should do as it ought."[72]

The campaign to get Charlie a fair hearing had influential supporters, with the *Sporting Life* saying that as a matter of fair play, he was entitled to a rehearing of the case. It pointed out that the owner of the horse in question, General Owen, supported

[72] Pall Mall Gazette, February 2nd, 1888

him and he had not been able to continue with the original criminal libel claim as his lawyer had refused to act.

The Jockey Club, however, had no intention of giving Charlie another hearing and instead set its sights on forcing its next target to sue for libel.

With Charlie banned, the press obsession with the story soon led to calls for an inquiry into Sir George Chetwynd's role in the scandal, alongside public fears that having severely punished Charlie, the establishment would protect its own.

Chetwynd's volatile character and hot temper had weakened his own position within the establishment. He had been a well-regarded member of the club and an effective steward, but for all that, he was not seen as sufficiently one of their own. He made no secret of the fact that he made his living from racing and he squandered some of his power and influence, in part gained through his friendship with the Prince of Wales, after he got embroiled in a public fight over who should accompany the Prince's mistress, Lillie Langtry.

As an American commentator noted: "Had the charges been made a few years ago the Prince of Wales would have been looked upon as party to such transactions. But it has been generally understood that since the affair in Hyde Park between Lord Lonsdale and Sir George Chetywnd, about Mrs Langtry, the latter had been excluded from the Marlborough House list."[73]

The loss of the protection he expected by virtue of his birth and rank was compounded when, after Durham's speech at the Gimcrack dinner, Chetwynd sent his brother, Captain Chetwynd, round to challenge Durham to a duel – "pistols-for-two and coffee-for-one"[74] – on the beaches of Calais. Illegal in England, duels were still fought in France at that time. He then wrote to the *Sportsman* and the Jockey Club to make public his demand for:

---

[73] St Louis Post Dispatch, December 28th, 1887
[74] The Mayfair Calendar, Horace Wyndham, 1925

"That satisfaction which every gentleman is entitled when insulted."

Despite several efforts by the Jockey Club to get Chetwynd to give an assurance that he would not duel with Durham, he refused to give one. If there was any wavering by its members, the cheap valour of such a challenge and the subsequent publication of the letter allowed Durham to stand firm in his drive for a public enquiry into his allegations. He argued that the matter had gone too far and that so much public interest had been aroused it was impossible to avoid a public inquiry.

Chetwynd did not want to go to court and asked the stewards to investigate behind closed doors. They declined and asked him again to sue for libel. He then went quiet, saying he had no intention of suing. So the Jockey Club called a meeting at 3.30pm on February 7th at Lord Hastings's London home in Bruton Street to discuss the "matters in dispute." It was, like all Jockey Club meetings, a private one, but the club took the unusual step of allowing the proceedings to be fully reported.[75]

The Jockey Club had sent all of its dukes and the gathering showed just how the aristocracy dominated racing. Along with four cabinet and ex-cabinet ministers, the attendees included Prince Soltykoff, Viscount Lascelles, Viscount Downe, the Duke of Richmond and Gordon, the Duke of Beaufort, the Duke of St Albans, the Duke of Westminster, the Duke of Portland, the Earl of Portsmouth, the Earl of Cork and Orrery, the Earl of Ellesmere, the Earl of Feversham, Earl Fitzwilliam, the Earl of Ilchester, the Earl of Rosslyn, the Earl of Westmorland, the Earl of Zetland, the Earl of Suffolk and Berkshire, the Earl of Hardwicke, Earl Howe, Lord Rosebery, Lord Falmouth, Lord Cadogan, Lord Alington, Lord Gerard, Lord Rendlesham, Lord Dorchester, Lord Penrhyn, Lord Calthorpe, Sir Reginald Graham and Sir R Jardine.

---

[75] The Times, February 8th, 1888

Without any hint of irony, the *Times* declared that such an assembly: "Might well be trusted, not only to decide upon the course which would be most to the advantage of the turf, but to force upon the disputants the fairest and most honourable methods of investigation."

At the meeting Chetwynd gave two reasons for not proceeding: he had not been named in Lord Durham's speech and so there was no libel, and that to sue in the courts meant the case would be submitted to a jury ignorant of turf matters and prejudiced against the accused parties. He said his legal advice was clear that he could not be forced to try and prove a negative and he wanted Durham to be made to lay a complaint and produce evidence before the stewards. But Durham was ready for him and said he was more than happy to remove all technical difficulties and promptly produced a letter naming Chetwynd, along with Charlie and Richard Sherrard.

> "I now state that the substance of my speech at the Gimcrack Dinner in York was to the effect that the horses in Sherrard's stable have shown constant and inexplicable changes of form, and that Wood, the jockey in that stable, has been in the habit of pulling them. I also accuse Sir George Chetwynd of having connived in serious malpractices which are contrary to the rules of racing."

During the meeting Lord Durham underlined his conviction that the whole issue must be investigated in the open and under the full scrutiny of the public eye. He referred again to the extensive comment about the running of certain horses and the conduct of their owners. "My wish was to bring this unsatisfactory state of things to a conclusion. It may be asked – why did you not draw the attention of the Stewards to the matter? My answer is, that as these insinuations and charges had been made in the press, in public, and on Newmarket Heath, I concluded that any investigation and reply to them should be made and conducted in full view of the public."

He asserted again that there had been no collusion with the Jockey Club before his speech. "It was made solely and entirely on my own responsibility, with the one object in view of the true interests of the Turf, and without any personal feelings whatever in respect of Sir George Chetwynd and Wood; also with the full intention of taking upon myself all responsibility for the matter and substance of my speech."

Chetwynd's second argument was that the court was a wholly unsuitable forum to decide racing disputes. "Naturally all I wish is to do what the Jockey Club think best. I am perfectly prepared to meet any charge against me and rebut it before any tribunal in the world, but I cannot go against my legal advisers, who say it is quite impossible I can go to a court of law. I am here ready to answer any questions that may be put to me by anybody in the Club."

But the Jockey Club members were ready for him and the Duke of Richmond and Gordon moved the resolution:

> "That in the opinion of the Jockey Club it is desirable that the matter in dispute between Sir George Chetwynd and Lord Durham should be taken to a court of law, with a view to the whole matter being referred to arbitration, as the Court, with the consent of the parties, may think fit."

It was carried unanimously. After they had comprehensively rejected a jury's ability to understand the complexities of racing, one member, Henry Chaplin, felt he had to write to the *Morning Post* to correct a comment he was reported as making.

"Speaking of the inconsistent running of racehorses, I am reported to have said, 'I cannot conceive a tribunal less calculated to arrive at a right decision upon such a complicated point than 12 shopkeepers of this city.' What I certainly intended to say, and what I am quite confident I did say, was this: 'Than, it may be, 12 tradesmen or shopkeepers of this city, not one of whom, perhaps, has ever seen a racehorse or been on a racecourse in his life.' Nothing could be further from my wishes or intentions than to speak slightingly or offensively of a class for whom no one entertains a higher respect than myself."

Chetwynd had been out manoeuvred. If he did not bring an action, the Jockey Club would expel him and he was left with no choice but to accept the resolution and submit the case to arbitration. The arbitrators would be men versed in all the manners and customs of racing men. They would also be drawn from the same Jockey Club to whom Chetwynd had first made his appeal.

Following the meeting, where Durham had made it clear his speech was also aimed at Charlie, the jockey made another attempt to clear his name. On February 14th he swore a statutory declaration in support of his application to renew his licence. He had no idea of the evidence against him and could only seek to address what he assumed was the reason for his banning – the alleged pulling of Success.

He pointed out that Success had not run well in his first two races with different jockeys. He had started second favourite at Lewes, where he had come third and the favourite, Primrose Boy, had won. He had then lost at Alexandra Park. He said that he had got away:

"Fairly at the start in both races and had every opportunity of winning each race, and should have won if the horse had been good enough, but he was not."

When Success won at Derby with a different jockey, the horse was carrying less weight and had an extra furlong to run on a straight and flat course.

Charlie's declaration was clear that he regularly put bets on for his owners, many of whom were Jockey Club members, and he evidently considered such acts of agency as part of his profession as a jockey.

"10. At Lewes I told Mr Robert Peck, I thought Success had a fair chance to win the race, and not having heard from General Williams, in reply to telegrams I sent to him, I asked Mr Peck to put £100 on the horse for the General.

11. I had told General Williams all about the horse's running at Lewes but thought he might perhaps have a chance at Alexandra Park, and if he thought so too, after seeing the entries, he could back him himself at the starting price, or telegraph to me at Alexandra Park on the morning of the race. I did not receive any telegram, and I do not know whether the General backed the horse, but I believe he did. I received a telegram from Lord Luggan on the morning of the race to back the horse for him for £200, if I thought he had a chance to win, and I asked an acquaintance of his lordship to put £100 only on."[76]

[76] The Yorkshire Post, February 27th, 1888

The *Otago Witness* was struck by how Charlie's declaration made it clear jockeys were openly mixed up in matters that they should have nothing to do with, but it seemed to be accepted practice. It was time, the paper argued, for the Jockey Club to put its own house in order.

> "It has long, of course, been common knowledge to race-goers that jockeys are no longer simply jockeys, whose duty is confined to weighing out and in and riding in the race. Whatever position any of them may secretly fulfil contrary to the rules of racing, they are enabled, without transgressing any rules, to act as agents for their masters for claiming racehorses and other matters, and apparently also to act as betting agents."[77]

The false position they occupied was been entirely the fault of the owners, it argued. If jockeys were in the habit of betting for their owners: "It stands to reason that they will also do so for themselves."

Given the class from which most jockeys spring, and their surroundings from their earliest years, it was not surprising that many go wrong; but, under ordinary circumstances, they are, taken all round, as honest as men of any other profession.

> "Under our present system the wonder is not that a few are dishonest, but that any are strong-minded enough to resist the many temptations so wantonly thrown in their way... when we find a jockey declaring (without any sense, apparently, of its incongruity, to use no stronger term) that he at his own discretion instructs

---

[77] Otago Witness, April 27th, 1888

Mr Peck to back a horse for £100 for a member of the Jockey Club, a sense of bewilderment falls upon us."[78]

The Jockey Club had attempted to stop jockeys betting in their own name during the early 1880s, to no avail. It only made clear that there was a prohibition which would be enforced during Durham's Gimcrack speech in December 1887, after the season when Charlie became champion jockey and after the running of Success.

Charlie finished his declaration with a direct appeal to the stewards for the return of his licence:

"I rode my first race about 17 years ago, when I adopted the occupation of jockey as a means of gaining my livelihood, and I have continued to follow it ever since. Last season (1887) I won more races than any other jockey in England. I am married and have a wife and five children. By the action of the Stewards of the Jockey Club in depriving me of my licence to ride, I am disgraced as a jockey, and am absolutely prevented from following my business as such, and I most humbly and earnestly pray the Stewards that they will give me the benefit of any doubt that exists as to the riding or running of Success, and that, under the circumstances herein stated, they will be pleased to re-consider their decision, and grant me annual licence to ride unconditionally; or in the alternative that they will be pleased to re-hear the case on General Williams's return to England, the witnesses being examined in my

---

presence face to face, and that in the meantime I may
be permitted to ride in races as a jockey."[79]

Charlie's lawyers, Greenfield and Cracknell, sent Lord
Hastings, the senior steward of the Jockey Club, a copy of the
statutory declaration saying they trusted that the stewards would
reconsider the case. The club's response was to publish the
voluminous correspondence.

On February 20th his lawyers followed up with an
undertaking that, if the stewards should see fit to grant Charlie
his annual licence, he would immediately take proceedings
against the *Licensed Victuallers' Gazette* and in those proceedings the
question whether he did or did not pull Success would be
judicially determined.

The appeal fell on deaf ears and it was left to Weatherby to
send another terse reply.

"Gentlemen,—The Stewards of the Jockey Club
desire me to acknowledge the receipt of your letters to
them and their enclosures, but in their opinion these do
not afford any grounds for reconsidering their decision
relative to the case of Success. – I am, gentlemen, your
obedient servant, Edward Weatherby."

Charlie's only option was to sue the *Licensed Victuallers' Gazette*
and Lord Durham for libel.

---

[79] The Yorkshire Post, February 27th, 1888

CHAPTER FIFTEEN

Derby Day, 1897

They're off

A great stillness descends over the crowd as they wait for the start and the invitations to bet grow fewer and fewer, until they cease altogether. The entertainments stop trying to attract customers. The crowds squeeze onto the rails with one common aim, to watch the Derby.

The start is far away from the stands, at the lowest point on the U shaped, left handed course. It is delayed as several horses, including Monterey, leap off before the signal. Nothing ruffles Galtee More as they are brought back to try again.

At 3.16pm Mr Coventry's flag finally falls and the shout goes up: "They're off."

The horses leap away and gallop up the hill in a line, like a cavalry charge: "In every way as exciting as that of the flower of Napoleon's cavalry at Waterloo." They climb the hill, a rise of 40 metres (the height of Nelson's Column) to the first corner, the highest point on the course.

Prime Minister starts to take an early lead on the outside. He is soon overtaken by Oakdene, running in blinkers. Charlie settles Galtee More into third place, on the inside by the rails. He decides to keep tucked in near the rails at this point in the race, but he knows he must stay alert as he runs the risk of finding himself boxed in and unable to position himself for the final dash for the finish.

At the top of the hill, History surges past Galtee More to take up third position, while Jack Watts on Velasquez starts to move through the field, gradually making up ground on the leaders.

The horses gallop round the sharp left handed turn at the top of the hill and start the downhill descent to the famous rails at Tattenham Corner. There is a ripple of concern across the crowd. It has been said that Galtee More will falter at this point.

Galtee More and Velasquez are pulling hard all the way.

"The Charles Wood Turf Libel Case"

CHAPTER SIXTEEN

The Great Turf Libel Case

The trial of Charlie's life

Charlie's libel proceedings against William H Cox, the publisher of the *Licensed Victuallers' Gazette and Hotel Courier*, came to court on June 18th, 1888. To clear his name and, he had been told, to get his licence back, he had been forced to sue the publisher over its false allegation that he had pulled Success. He claimed £5,000 [£640,000] in damages for the injury to his reputation and the loss of his licence. He also issued a separate writ against Lord Durham, which was set be heard later in a separate action.

Charlie had placed his future in the hands of the legal system but, as the case proceeded, it was clear it would not protect him. The evidence, much of it rumour and suspicion, allowed by the judge, regardless of Charlie's own evidence and even the decision of the jury, would do him irreparable harm. As Sir Frances Lawley later commented in *The Bench and the Jockey Club*, it quickly became clear that the trial was presided over by a judge with no knowledge of racing but a clear interest in preserving the superiority of the master over his servant.

On its face, the libel was quite simple, contained in the verb 'pulled'. Did Charlie 'pull' Success – "when Charley Wood nearly pulled its head off on each occasion?" The *Licensed Victuallers' Gazette* had a reputation for sailing close to the wind with its scurrilous gossip and it occasionally tilted at leading figures in racing. Some years previously Matthew Dawson had brought an action for criminal libel against the paper's then publisher, accusing the *Gazette* of: "Imputing gross profligacy and misconduct in doctoring Lord Falmouth's horse entered for the Cesarewitch." In that case, the publisher had quickly backed down.

As he prepared his case Charlie was already at a disadvantage as his usual lawyer, solicitor George Lewis, along with the leading barrister and well known racing enthusiast Sir Charles Russell QC, had been instructed by Durham to act for Cox, at Durham's expense. Despite the continued denials of collusion, it was clear that Durham viewed the case as a fishing exercise to help his advisers prepare his defence against Charlie and Chetwynd's libel actions. Charlie's lawyers, Greenfield and Cracknell, instructed another leading barrister of the day, Sir Henry James QC, to act for Charlie.

On the first day, the Lord Chief Justice, Lord Coleridge, settled down to preside over the most high profile jury trial of the year, savouring the fact that the hearing had become a social event, with the great and the good squeezed into court to enjoy the spectacle of 'The Great Turf Libel Case'. Lord Coleridge even invited his wife and daughter to attend.

The case was heard in the largest court in the Royal Courts on the Strand in London, but had it been five times larger, it would still not have accommodated all those who arrived to watch. The court room resembled the first day of Ascot, packed with racing aristocracy, among them some key players in Charlie's story. Durham sat in the first row of the public gallery and Chetwynd was also in court every day.

The party atmosphere was enhanced when the first decision was to bounce a licensed victualler from the jury on the grounds of possible bias.

The *South Wales Echo* reported on the enormous public support for Charlie throughout the trial under the heading 'The

Hero of the Hour'. Each day a large crowd awaited his arrival, when his "dapper little form" would appear about a quarter of an hour before the court convened, always dressed in sombre black and showing a little white at the neck with a narrow black necktie "tied with irreproachable neatness." Once settled in court, Charlie sat quietly throughout and the only signs he gave of any interest in the proceedings were the occasional puckering of his forehead and rolling of his eyes.

> "Whether in the witness-box subjected to the running fire of cross-examination, listening to the evidence of others, or to the scathing criticism of Sir Charles Russell, who did not spare the lash... his attitude has been that of an intelligent spectator. A very cool hand he has shown himself, and coolness has been one of the most prominent features of all the witnesses in this remarkable case."[80]

The *Echo* said that, all the way through the trial, the crowd showed the "utmost curiosity" in Charlie. At lunch and when the court adjourned on each day, the corridors were lined with people waiting for him to walk by.

> "And as he passed along these people fell in and followed up the hero of the hour, whose diminutive figure was shut in and lost to view amongst the crowd."

The rest of the attendees did not fare so well. Large crowds gathered around the entrance to the Law Courts and when the witnesses and others connected with the trial "were shot out into the Strand every afternoon, they would rather indicate that public opinion ran in the direction of assuming that the turfites,

---

[80] South Wales Echo, June 29th, 1888

although they included lords and ladies, owners, trainers, and jockeys, and enterprising gentlemen who got their living by betting, were a very shady lot."[81]

Sir Henry James opened on behalf of Charlie in his usual vivacious manner: "Succeeding without much action, but by the well managed inflection off a well-managed voice, to impress even the very small details upon the attention of the court and jury."[82]

If the intention had been to annoy Durham, the choice of James was inspired. The Earl had refused to speak to him since the barrister appeared for his wife in Durham's high profile and ultimately unsuccessful attempt to get his marriage nullified.

The eldest twin son of the second Earl of Durham, he had inherited his title in 1879. He married the "excessively" shy beauty, Ethel Elizabeth Louisa Milner, in 1882. By 1885 he was suing to have the marriage annulled after having Ethel committed to a mental hospital, Barnwood Asylum, near Gloucester, where she stayed until her death in 1931. Durham claimed she had been insane when he married her.

The week long case had been a sensation, with the court packed every day and the evidence picked over in great detail by the newspapers. Durham had sought to prove insanity, but his grounds were weak. They included the claims that she occasionally refused to speak, dance or eat, and loved going for long walks.

Sir Henry had been ruthless in his cross examination. During the hearing it transpired that Ethel had panicked on her wedding night, when Durham had almost dragged her up the steps into his house.

The judge had found that on the third night Durham:

---

[81] The Queenslander, August 18th, 1888
[82] North Eastern Daily Gazette, June 19th, 1888

"Did not show that tenderness and consideration towards his bride that her condition called for. His threat to leave her and send her back to her mother was highly calculated to disturb her mind; and his whole statement showed how little he knew how to win his young wife's affection by gentleness and patience."[83]

Before the marriage he had shown Ethel off in society and been congratulated on her beauty and modesty. To then claim she had been an 'imbecile' before he married her was thrown out as untenable.

As a result, Durham could neither divorce Ethel nor produce a legitimate heir. While she languished in the asylum he spent most of his life in a relationship with a famous dancer, Letty Lind. They had a son in 1892, who could never inherit his title as he was illegitimate. When Durham died in 1928, he was succeeded in the earldom by his younger twin brother, Frederick.

The case haunted Durham throughout his life and just before Chetwynd's libel action against him came to court in 1889 he brought criminal libel proceedings against a paper that said he had been cruel to Ethel.

In his opening speech Sir Henry James denounced the Jockey Club for refusing Charlie his licence without permitting him to come face to face with his accusers or giving him any opportunity to defend himself against their accusations. As a result the jockey, who had reached the highest position in his profession, had been forced into court to vindicate his character. For the first time, he said, the stewards of the Jockey Club would be brought to book for having practically destroyed the professional career of an honourable and successful man behind closed doors and when

---

[83] Carlisle Patriot, March 13th, 1885

the jury heard the evidence they would acquit Charlie of the accusations.

During the course of the day's proceedings it became clear that, while the defendant had the sympathy and support of some members the Jockey Club, the *vox populis* was with Charlie. The judge was often compelled to bang his gavel and threaten to clear the court if the spectators continued to laugh and applaud the statements of the jockey's barrister and witnesses. His problems started with the first witness, jockey Thomas Weldon, who soon reduced the court to laughter when he baldly stated: "I have heard of Wood pulling horses, but that is said of all jockeys that I know about!"

William Robinson, also a jockey, then took the stand. He said that he thought Charlie did all he could to win and the talk of jockeys pulling horses came from the lower classes. He could not say whether jockeys belonged to the upper or lower class – which also made the spectators laugh – but he had not heard jockeys say that Charlie pulled horses. He added that jockeys often got accused behind their backs and he knew people had said it about his own riding.

On June 23rd, Captain Arthur de Vere Smith, 38th Regiment of Foot, a compact, natty figure, well known in racing circles, "showed to advantage in the witness-box," according to the *Aberdeen Press and Journal*. As he had been present both at Lewes and Alexandra Park, he was called to give evidence to the running of Success. At Lewes he had backed Primrose Boy, the winner. Success was running well and looked like winning and about 200 or 300 yards from the post, he said, Charlie began to ride hard, punishing the horse with his whip. Asked whether there was any evidence for saying that Charlie rode unfairly, Captain De Very Smith replied: "Certainly not." He also saw the finish of the race at Alexandra Park and gave similar testimony as to Charlie's riding.

However, his standing as a truthful witness took a knock when Sir Charles Russell drew on his extensive racing knowledge to ask him if he had been a "bookmaker's clerk in the ring", which he denied. As he made his way back to his seat, the captain had a whispered conversation with Sir Henry James and then, as he stood in the gangway between the eminent counsel, he confessed that he had indeed booked bets for his partner George Hodgson. To the amusement of the court, he added that, in his view, that did not mean he was a bookmaker's clerk.

Robert Peck, a well-known trainer, also appeared for Charlie. A clean shaven and well dressed man in a white waistcoat and white tie, he was a pleasant and amiable witness. He thought Charlie rode Success quite honestly. He had commented to Charlie after the race that it had been a rather tame finish and Charlie had replied: "I drove the horse as hard as I could but he was dead tired, and so was I."

Charlie did not ride flogging finishes, unlike Fred Archer, and this was now coming back to bite him. The trainer said he had commented at the time that if he had known that he would have thrown his umbrella at Charlie, but he never intended to impugn the jockey's reputation and he attached little value to the talk in turf circles. He had heard a number of rumours of improper riding by other jockeys, but having seen the jockeys he paid no heed to them. He ended by saying he was quite certain that Charlie had never pulled a horse.

When Charlie came to the stand his evidence started well. In a 17-year career he had ridden in over 2,000 races and had 631 winners. He had ridden for some of the biggest names in racing: General Peel, Lord Stamford, Mr George Payne, Mr Crawford, Prince Batthyany, the Dukes of Beaufort, Westminster, Hamilton, and St Albans, along with Lords Cadogan and Cardigan.

He was asked: "Have any of those noblemen and gentlemen for whom you have ridden made any complaint about your riding for them on the ground that your riding was dishonest?" Given that it would soon become clear that, despite hiring private detectives to try and dig up some evidence to use against Charlie, the whole defence case was based on suspicion and rumour, it was ironic that Russell objected to that question as not being evidence.

Charlie said he did not interfere with Success, but the horse had changed its legs several times going down the hill at Lewes and started to hang.

He did not think much of Success as a racehorse. He had run badly in his trials and Charlie thought he better suited a straight level course such as Derby, where the horse later won with a different jockey, rather than a rounded or hilly one such as Lewes or the heavy going at Alexandra Park.

He had put £10 on Success to win at Lewes; he had nothing to gain from Success losing at Alexandra Park and had not bet on the horse at Derby.

Russell stood to start his cross examination and Charlie had an easy, offhand way of answering his questions which annoyed the eminent lawyer. However, Russell was a skilful advocate and a regular race goer who bet frequently and the champion jockey was about to learn one of the hard lessons about being subjected to a forensic cross examination as he sought to downplay his income.

During his evidence, Charlie said that in the four years up to losing his licence he earned about £4,000 a year. "Does that include your betting" responded Russell and Charlie was forced to reply that he had "not reckoned it up." He finally admitted to a racing income of £5,000 to £6,000 a year. Russell was unrelenting, "And you keep carriages and have servants and grooms?" Charlie made the court laugh again when he replied that he kept a boy to brighten and blacken his boots.

He was then made to list his substantial property holdings. He owned Lowther House opposite the Jockey Club gates in Newmarket, where he lived with his family; the Greyhound and Black Horse hotels; Chetwynd House and stables, which he had built and had accommodation for 48 horses; two cottages in St Mary's Square in the town and some smaller cottages.

He also had £4,000 invested in the Argyle Wharf Cooperage at Limehouse, which paid him 18 per cent, owned an additional 35 acres and stables let as a training yard at Cheveley, and had £12,000 invested in government bonds. He kept two hunters and regularly bought and sold horses. Which all generated him an annual income much closer to £10,000 [£1.2m], without taking into account his betting.

In *"Master" & Men Pink 'un Yesterdays*, John Bennion Booth recounts the moment when, as Charlie was undergoing the heavy cross-examination on his income, one of his barristers, Sir Frank Lockwood, made a diversion by complaining that the jockey's accusers, including Durham, Sporting Times journalist John Corlett and others "of influence and position" were sitting in the seats reserved for counsel for the Crown, which might lead to a bias in the minds of the jury. Lord Coleridge quickly ordered them all out.

During the adjournment for lunch, Corlett told Lockwood that, as he had had him thrown him out of his ringside seat, he expected some return.

"A few days later the return arrived in the shape of a pen and ink sketch of the Lord Chief Justice, in jockey costume, with the note – The Lord Chief Justice, three months after hearing that Charles Wood made ten thousand a year as a jockey."

Lockwood had added a handwritten comment: "How do you think the Chief would do."

LORD COLERIDGE.
By Sir Frank Lockwood.

"Master" and Men

Russell's cross examination successfully created the impression of a jockey, still regarded as a servant in the 1880s, awash with money and with no clear explanation of its source.

It was clear throughout the case that the judge, Durham and Russell were outraged that a mere servant (although they did not say it in court, in this case a servant who was illegitimate and born in a slum) had risen to become as wealthy as his masters. In his opening speech to the jury later in the case, Russell went so far as to declare: "In the primitive days of racing, the trainer was the groom and the jockey a servant; nowadays the trainer is the master of the owner, and the jockey master of them both."[84]

---

[84] Sporting Times, June 30th, 1888

The Sheffield and Rotherham Independent picked up on the large sums jockeys had started to earn.

> "Only the professional men who live to clutch the prizes of their callings, and very few business men, are able to cap the tales told by "Charley Wood's" bank book, with its annual turnover of £12,000, and possibly £15,000 [£1.9m]. This distinguished gentleman acknowledges to an income besides which that of England's Prime Minister becomes pale, and which exceeds that of a Lord Chancellor... When we consider the ceaseless labour that a successful lawyer, doctor or author has to undergo to earn anything approaching to the proceeds of Mr Wood's brief and exciting experiences in the saddle, it must be confessed that there is a good deal of disparity. Both between the sums of life and the trouble it takes to clutch them. A popular jockey only has to open his mouth and they drop in."[85]

James stood and tried to repair the damage. Charlie was encouraged to emphasise his humble background. That he started his professional life at a very young age with no financial assistance, had a large family to provide for and lived modestly, only spending £600 to £700 a year. To explain his wealth, he also listed some of the large presents he had been given by grateful owners, including over £1,000 [£119,000] for each of his two Derby wins. The Duchess of Montrose – who raced under the pseudonym 'Mr Manton' as women could not own racehorses at that time – had given him £400 for winning the Royal Hunt Cup.

---

[85] Sheffield and Rotherham Independent, June 23rd, 1888

The court did not discuss the presents given to other jockeys, but it was well known in the racing world that, for Fred Archer, the presents had often been much bigger. In 1928 Alexander Scott, the author of *Turf Memories of Sixty Years*, was reminiscing about the 1882 St Leger with a Press Association reporter before that year's race:

> "I saw the great Fred Archer ride six winners of the St Leger and on one of them, Dutch Oven, he rode probably the hardest race of his career. I watched the filly being unsaddled after the race, and have never seen a more distressed winner anywhere. Archer had flogged Dutch Oven severely and the reason was that a fortune for himself and two others depended on his winning. John Hammond and Arthur Cooper, two big commissioners of the period, won £40,000 and £20,000 respectively over Dutch Oven's victory. Between them they were said to have given Archer £15,000 [£1.7m] as a present."[86]

General Owen Williams, also a member of the Jockey Club, stepped up to help his jockey. It was his horse that everyone was claiming Charlie had pulled and he told the court he was certain that was not the case. He had known Charlie for 10 years, and had employed him as his jockey for four. He had asked Charlie to enter Success at Lewes and Alexandra Park. The horse had already lost at Newmarket and Sandown. At Sandown he had backed the horse and lost his money.

At Alexandra Park he said he had backed the horse for a place. After the race he decided to get rid of Success and gave instructions that, as the horse was a bad one, he did not want him returned to the stables. He was pleased when he went to Derby to

---

[86] Coventry Evening Telegraph, August 29th, 1928

hear that the horse was sold for £150 and it made it clear that Charlie's conduct at Alexandra Park had met with his decided approval. In his view, Success had the advantage of carrying 7lb less weight when he won at Derby, and was better suited to that course.

He added that the in-and-out running of a horse was a regular occurrence with no dishonesty involved. A horse's health and the condition of the ground could make a material difference in its running.

He had made no complaint against Charlie's riding and had not heard any suggestion that Charlie had pulled the horse. The general said he had not found racing at all a paying game, but he had heard rumours similar to those against Charlie about every jockey except John Osborne. He got a round of applause when he added: "There was a number of dishonest people who were incapable of believing that there was any honesty in other people."

Sir John Astley, another famous racing name at that time, appeared for Charlie and said he had seen Success run at Alexandra Park and saw nothing extraordinary in it and it was a common thing for horses to change their form. Success's trainer, Martin Gurry, also supported Charlie and said Success had been beaten on his merits and Charlie had ridden to win.

But Charlie's case seemed to stumble, as Russell stated again and again that Charlie was dishonest, without being asked to produce evidence to prove his assertion. In nearly every instance he put a leading question to witnesses: "Have you not heard that Wood had a bad reputation?" Much more loaded than the more neutral: "Has Wood a bad reputation?"

In a later related case, when Durham sought to amend his defence against the libel action being brought by Charlie, the judges were highly critical of the way the Lord Chief Justice had let it happen.

As a result, even the witnesses called to give evidence of Charlie's good character ended up admitting under cross examination that they had heard rumours to the contrary. For example, when the judge at Lewes races, JF Clarke, was called on Charlie's behalf he stated that there was nothing in his riding to show that he had ridden unfairly. But under Russell's cross examination he admitted that he had heard "rumours that Wood sometimes did not try to win."

Sir Charles Russell's opening speech for the defence twisted the knife. He told the jury that they had to decide whether Charlie had been libelled and, if so, what the damages should be. He said he could not see much call for high damages as even Charlie's own witnesses had confirmed that he did not have a good reputation and that he was widely said to pull horses.

He called attention to Charlie's large income, saying that under the Jockey Club scheme which set the fees jockey could claim for a ride, Charlie would have earned in the region of £1,900 [£240,000] a year. It would be for the jury, he said, to decide whether his income, which was well in excess of the set fees, was fairly earned.

He then tried to plant the defence's flag on the moral high ground, claiming that the case was more than just a question of libel, and that the reputation of the whole sport hung in the balance. It was the duty of those who thought racing deserved better to rally behind the few trying to rid the sport of its corrupting forces. There were those who believed that racing was an "ignoble sport" and anyone coming into contact with it was inevitably corrupted. But racing was the most popular sport in the country and it should be protected from those who sought to destroy it. "All who believed that the sport might be so conducted as to be a healthy recreation," he said, "could not fail to take an interest in this case, the history of which discloses an earnest attempt on the part of those who had regard for the true and manly interest of the sport to attempt to purify the atmosphere of it which is so justly described as foul."

The defence struggled throughout the case as they had no evidence that Charlie pulled horses. The best they could produce was a stable boy, Evans, who, to laughter in court, said he: "Knew when Wood the jockey 'pulled' a horse by the manner he sat upon it." He claimed he had seen him do it in several races.

Evans was followed by a procession of the great and the good of racing, particularly members of the Jockey Club. With no need to supply any evidence to back up their claims, they all made assertions about Charlie's reputation. Lord Marcus Beresford, official starter for the Jockey Club, simply stated he had a bad reputation. Major Egerton, the official handicapper, stated that: "As regards the pulling of horses and general manipulation of the Turf, Wood's character was as bad as it could be." His own reputation as the handicapper depended on his judgement of a horse's ability. If he got it wrong, he might well look to blame the jockey.

One of the witnesses against Charlie was jockey Frederick Barrett, who was then leading the list of winning jockeys and would become champion jockey that year, a position he almost certainly owed to Charlie's suspension. He testified that, contrary to Charlie's claims that the horse Success was no good, he had been in a race where the horse had won and he was "quick on his legs." Barrett would also win the Derby that year on Ayrshire and later trained in Jevington, before Charlie settled there.

Charlie's legal team countered with a lengthy list of aristocrats prepared to stand by him, including the Duke of

Beaufort, the Marquis of Hartington and the Earl of Westmorland, who all testified that they placed no credence in the rumours against Charlie.

Beaufort in particular stood as a great friend of Charlie's during the case, staying in court the whole time, sitting next to his solicitor. Hartington said that it was often commented that jockeys "always knew better than others" which made the spectators laugh again, and allowed Russell to return to his favourite theme in reply: "They took it upon themselves to be masters instead of servants."

The Duke of Portland was one of the last witnesses called on behalf of Charlie. He said he had continued to employ Charlie until his licence was revoked, believing him an honest jockey.

In a controversial move, Russell tried to wrong foot Portland by pulling out a letter he had written to Durham addressed to 'Dear Jacko,' (Durham's nickname) in which he had stated that all jockeys were rascals.

Under cross examination the Duke did not blink. "I meant the whole class of jockeys."

"If jockeys are damned thieves you have put up a good many damn thieves," countered Russell. The spectators laughed when Duke replied, "I certainly have."

As his parting shot he said he had heard it stated that lawyers were all thieves but he did not believe that either and sat down to more loud laughter and gavel banging by the judge.

The *St James's Gazette* later poured scorn on Durham for producing the letter:

> "The discussion between Sir Charles Russell, Sir Henry James, and Lord Coleridge about the Duke of Portland's famous letter to Lord Durham has excited a good deal of interest in legal and other circles. Of course in law, if Sir Charles Russell considered that the

production of the letter was likely to help his client's case on a point on which there may be… a difference of professional opinion – he was bound to produce it. On the other hand, the question whether it was a chivalrous or creditable act on the part of Lord Durham to produce the letter is a perfectly distinct one, and one on which there is hardly room for two opinions. If Lord Durham had produced the letter in self-defence in a case of his own, his conduct would have been doubtful; under the existing circumstances it was deplorable."

In his summing up, Russell developed his theme that part of the problem in racing, and society as a whole, was that the lower classes no longer seemed to know their place.

George Lambton, Durham's brother, reported later that Russell has concluded, "The turf is much changed from the old days when the jockey was the servant, and the owner the master. Now you see the jockey getting fatter and richer" (Wood was always very prosperous looking) "and" pointing to the General, "the owners thinner and poorer."[87]

It was cheap blow, especially as General Williams, the owner of Success, was ill and extremely thin at the time of the trial.

After hearing all the evidence, the bookies were backing a win for Charlie – until the Lord Chief Justice started his summing up. It was so heavily weighted towards the defendant they changed their mind and started to offer odds on William Cox to win.

The judge went in hard on Charlie's reputation, to the point where he told the jury that they must give the stewards of the Jockey Club credit for common sense and understanding. He said they would not withdraw Charlie's licence simply in consequence

---

[87] Men and Horses I have Known, George Lambton, 1924

of the *Licensed Victuallers' Gazette* claim that he pulled horses. The fact that they withheld it could not be the direct and reasonable result of the libel but the result of their separate investigation.

He ignored the fact that no evidence had been brought to court to back that assertion up, and soon warmed to his theme. Ignoring the law's usual requirement for proof and its deep mistrust of hearsay, he said:

"Dealing with the question of Wood's reputation, high authority once said, 'Most men are such as most men think them.'"

There was, he said, not one single witness who had been called for either side who did not admit that they had heard the character of the plaintiff reflected upon. He proposed only to read the evidence of four witnesses who were officials of the Jockey Club. "They were four men of unblemished reputation, and the jury had heard their statements as to the bad reputation of the defendant."

He went so far as to state that Charlie's supporters only stuck with him as there was "no proof on oath" that he pulled horses. James challenged that statement, but the judge stuck fast, saying that was how he interpreted their evidence. He also commented on the delay in Charlie bringing proceedings, and questioned whether the jockey had shown the: "Anxiety to get rid of the charge that he pulled horses which might be expected of an innocent man," ignoring the fact that he had started criminal libel proceedings and then lost his original legal team to Durham.

Despite the judge's best efforts, the final verdict absolved Charlie of pulling Success. But there was a sting in the tail when the jury went on to award him one farthing in damages – the smallest amount possible.

The *St James Gazette* made clear it was disturbed by the way the judge had allowed the case to proceed.

> "Wood obtained only nominal damages because a dozen persons familiar with racing were ready to come and say that he was generally reputed to be in the habit of pulling horses. What does such evidence really come to? It is avowedly hearsay. It might well be – it may or may not be in the present case – mere scandalous gossip derived from the possibly malicious inventions of two or three interested persons. Is it right that a man should be deprived of the possibility of vindicating his character from a definite charge made against him, because a certain number of people are prepared to say that his reputation is bad?"[88]

The editorial prompted a highly unusual letter to the paper from one of the jurors. He said he agreed with the paper's view, even though it differed from most of its contemporaries, that the conclusion of this case was not quite satisfactory, and for the reasons given by the paper, but he was surprised that they did not infer that the verdict was to some extent compromise. He offered his view on how it was arrived at:

> "When the jury retired they were as nearly equally divided between plaintiff and defendant as a jury of eleven can be; that is to say, there were five for each, and one, possibly the wisest, who seemed to have an open mind on the subject. It should be noted that the judge, probably by instinct, brought his remarks to conclusion at one o'clock; and the jury were ushered into their dismal, barely furnished den just when lunch

---

[88] St James's Gazette, June 30th, 1888

begins to have a direct bearing upon any other subject which may happen to engage the attention of businessmen. It was presently discovered that Wood was handicapped more heavily than even Major Egerton would have considered necessary 'for the protection of the public' by the fact that one of his most conscientious opponents had brought with him a packet of sandwiches, which, whilst they irritated the digestive organs, tended to anaesthetise the consciences of some who were sandwichless."

The juror said nicotine, through the use of pipes and cigarettes, helped to equalise the weights, and the two parties proceeded to a formal disputation. The friends of the plaintiff differed considerably in their attachment to his cause, and estimated his reputation at various sums from a farthing to five thousand pounds.

"Their esteem for him seemed to me to vary inversely as their respect for the Lord Chief Justice, but I will not vouch for the accuracy of this formula. However, they held together, and after nearly two hours – for it was a matter of conscience and great principles were involved – they perceived some signs of giving on the other side. Hunger began to do its work, especially on some who looked like hearty eaters but had neither food nor tobacco."

At one point it was suggested that they should give no verdict, until it was pointed out that they would lose their special juror's fee of nine guineas apiece. "This horrid idea produced a painful impression on all, and acted as a powerful solvent on the scruples of some."

They reached a position where they agreed they were willing to accept the opinion of the majority, which now appeared to incline to the plaintiff's side.

> "Wood's principal opponent, by the personal efforts of one of our side, was brought to the point of agreeing to a verdict for the plaintiff without damages... The result is, in my opinion, creditable to the common sense of the jury collectively, and a fair specimen of popular as distinguished from ideal justice. Juries' justice is, perhaps, not the highest conceivable; but I have come to the conclusion that it is often the best attainable. The judge several times congratulated himself that he had not to decide the case, and towards the end of his summing up I fancy the plaintiff must have agreed with him. The jury might easily have come to a worse conclusion; and though I think I could have done better myself, that perhaps is the individual opinion of nearly every... *One of the Jurors*"[89]

Charlie had won by a very short head and Cox presented him with his farthing immediately after the case. A large crowd of supporters followed him out of the building to a waiting cab and cheered as he drove off. He stopped to pay the coin into his account at the Prudential Bank on Ludgate Hill and left for Newmarket.

The judge refused to award him costs despite his victory, and while William Cox could look to Lord Durham to write the cheque, Charlie had to meet his own costs estimated in excess of £2,000 [£252,000]. Sir Henry James's brief alone was marked 600 guineas, with a "refresher" of 50 guineas per day.

---

[89] St James's Gazette, July 2nd, 1888

The *Licensed Victuallers' Gazette's* poison pen had been poised to let rip after the case. In an article headlined 'Wood v Ourselves' on June 22nd it had to sit on its hands, as it did not want to be held in contempt of court. "We have no intention of commenting on the Great Turf Libel Case… at this stage in the proceedings. Such a grave indiscretion would not only compromise our dignity, but would distinctly prejudice our interests."

A week later, as the case was dragging on, it was annoyed that it could not render a full account and was left to state that the case was an important investigation into the mysteries of racing and would have a "vast impact upon the future of racing." It looked forward to enlightening the public on "the real part we ourselves have played in the matter."

By its next edition, on July 6th, it was left picking up the pieces after its defeat. "If the revelations have not been as startling and sensational as some persons expected them to be, they must, at any rate, be pronounced remarkable."

The premier jockey in England, it said, had come forward to defend his reputation and had been awarded a farthing.

> "We have won a complete and triumphant moral
> victory, and we can, without egotism or boastfulness,
> lay the flattering unction to our souls that we have done
> something towards that purification of the turf which
> all good and honest sportsmen desire to see."

The paper was left praising Russell, but neglected to say his services were paid for by Durham. It also praised the Lord Chief Justice for the singularly lucid and impartial way he summed up the case for the jury, contrary to the general view that he had been heavily weighted towards the defence and had displayed a woeful ignorance about racing.

After the case, the *Sporting Life* awarded Charlie the nickname "nutmeg – on account of the difficulty experienced in cracking him," and concluded that he had faced the music with considerable pluck. His dismissal of Durham's Gimcrack speech as an after dinner effort and therefore not worthy of notice, "was delicious."

Sir George Chetwynd was said to be openly jubilant. If Durham's defence consisted of the same generalities, he would also lose the libel case Chetwynd was bringing against him.

The general view was that, unless the Jockey Club had some strong trump cards to play in the next cases, it must be getting uneasy – a fact clearly indicated by Durham's attempt to amend his defence before Charlie's libel action against him came to court. An attempt that spectacularly backfired.

Durham's defence to Charlie's libel action was justification, claiming the truth of the words complained of. After the result in *Wood v Cox*, he sought to add a paragraph to his statement of defence to the effect that at the date of the publication of the libel the plaintiff, Charlie, was: "A person of such general reputation that he was not injuriously affected by the libel."

The High Court refused to give permission and the case eventually came before Mr Justice Manisty and Mr Justice Hawkins in the Court of Appeal on August 9th, 1888. Sir Henry James appeared for Charlie.

The judges were shocked at Durham's audacity. Manisty asked Durham's lawyer: "Do you mean that a witness is to be called into the box to say of a principal in the case, 'Yes, his general reputation is bad' and that it is to end there?"

Durham's barrister replied: "That was the course followed in *Wood v Cox* in connection with a large number of witnesses."

Manisty was outraged. "All I can say is that anything more likely to lead to injustice I cannot conceive than a witness should come into the box and give evidence that a man's general reputation is very bad. Give a dog a bad name and hang him, and there is an end to him. I cannot conceive anything so opposed to all ideas I have of justice and fair dealing."[90]

Durham's lawyer tried again. "I will take this illustration: suppose a thief, having been convicted forty or fifty times of felony, is wrongfully charged with having stolen a particular man's watch; if it is shown that he enjoyed the reputation of being a reputed thief, the fact that he is charged with a specific felony..."

Manisty cut him short. "You try the case apart from all previous convictions, and do not even allow the jury to know that he has been convicted."

He said that the asked-for amendment effectively sought to say that Charlie generally pulled horses and what a frightful issue that would raise in law. If such a plea could not be pleaded as to particular horses, it could hardly be pleaded generally, he said. It was like saying: "It is true you did not commit this larceny, but you stole my horse."

He concluded that the idea that they should exclude a plaintiff from damages in a particular case because he had misconducted himself in other particular matters went beyond anything that had ever before been suggested.

Mr Justice Hawkins, a racing authority, agreed with his colleague, saying that if it was the practice to put rumour on the record, the trials for slander and libel would be interminable and they would be decided, in nine cases out of ten, not on the merits of the case but upon prejudice.

In *The Bench and the Jockey Club*, Sir Francis Lawley highlighted the judges' concern that Charlie had been damned by racecourse rumour, which spares nobody, and his reputation had been simply sneered away.

---

[90] The York Herald, August 10th, 1888

"If the new law inaugurated in *Wood v Cox* is established, I would suggest that in every room in the High Court of Judicature, and throughout the law courts of the United Kingdom 'Give a dog a bad name and hang him!' be inscribed in letters three feet long."

He said that he was brought up with the understanding that every Englishman charged with any offence was held to be innocent until proved to the contrary.

"Henceforth, according to the new doctrine laid down in *Wood v Cox*, a plaintiff who has been shamefully libelled is to be refused redress at his libeller's hands if as a boy or a young man it can by any means be shown that he was suspected of poaching, robbing fruit orchards or stealing eggs."

The establishment, despite this ruling, kept after Charlie. As 1889 arrived, he might have assumed that he would get his licence back as he had won his libel case. But he was refused again. To add insult to injury, on February 12th, 1889 his appeal against being left to pay his own costs in *Wood v. Cox*, despite having won, was refused.

The Master of the Rolls, Lord Esher, resolutely ignored the concerns Manisty and Hawkins had over relying on rumour and hearsay and damned Charlie once more: "The sole issue before the jury was whether the plaintiff has pulled a horse on two occasions, and the jury found that he did not pull the horse on either occasion. The verdict is conclusive on that issue" but Esher then concluded: "A man with such a character as Wood had no right to bring the action, and acted oppressively in doing so, and therefore good cause existed for depriving him of costs."

Lawley was outraged at the injustice. With the exception of Manisty and Hawkins, he said, every judge before whom any proceeding connected with Charlie had thus far come seemed determined to give him a bad name and hang him.

Alexander Scott in his later memoir *Turf Memories of Sixty Years* was in no doubt of Charlie's innocence of the charge. "I have always sympathised with Wood in this affair. To begin with, the colt Success was one of the softest animals I ever saw on a racecourse." He says at Sandown, when Charlie was not the jockey, he backed Success and: "Naturally took an interest in his running. The colt ran soft. At Lewes I backed Success again, thinking the easy downhill stretch from the start would suit him better, but Success sprawled all over the course coming down it, and no jockey on earth could have straightened him to win his race."

He adds: "Yet several excellent judges of racing in the ordinary way were foolish enough to say then that Wood ought to have won. I fancy their pockets were speaking loudest on that occasion."

Scott also saw Success run at Alexandra Park, where he was well backed. "After the race I was standing with a little group in the paddock comprising Martin Gurry, Billy Marshall, and another racing enthusiast. The latter remarked to Gurry, 'You are going to lose your horse.' ... 'I don't worry about that,' Gurry replied. 'I would rather have a suit of the General's old clothes as a present than I would the horse, if he wanted to give me one'; which showed unmistakably that, good judge as Martin Gurry was, he thought very little indeed of Success."

Success was sold to Charley White and, says Scott, he bought him believing that the colt had not been a trier previously.

"When he sent Success on to Derby and won a race…
no doubt he thought his assumption correct.
Unfortunately, many other people did so too, but the
facts were simple enough at the time to me. The three
previous races had sharpened Success up a bit, so that
when he came to the very easy course at Derby – the
second easiest six furlongs in England in my opinion –
everything was in his favour. He never did much good
after this."

CHAPTER SEVENTEEN

Derby Day, 1897

To Tattenham Corner

© Illustrated London News Ltd/Mary Evans

The horses gallop on down to Tattenham Corner, Epsom's legendary sweeping left handed turn. Charlie has arrived at the critical point in the battle. The decisions he makes here will win, or lose, him the race.

As they approach, the rails round away from them like the half-circle of some huge circus ring.

"On the left, as the jockeys ride, are the rails, those famous rails which we have heard so much of, and whose fame has extended to the uttermost parts of the earth. Rails which have actually became historical, rising to a dignity and eminence far beyond their mere timber-carrying capacity. No rails will ever rise to the dignity of Tattenham Corner rails. Their position is not assailable."[91]

Charlie has already decided to position himself on the rails. If he drifts wide he will lose ground, ground that takes a lot of making up in the final run for the finish.

He has ridden tight to those rails to his advantage before. The way he cut so close that he grazed his boot on his way to winning the 1883 Derby by a head with St Blaise is the stuff of racing legend.

As he approaches at full gallop he positions Galtee More just where he wants him, and he negotiates the corner close to the white rails in third place, with Oakdene still leading and History now second.

---

[91] Sporting Sketches, Nat Gould, 1900

THE ILLUSTRATED LONDON NEWS

REGISTERED AT THE GENERAL POST-OFFICE FOR TRANSMISSION ABROAD.

No. 2618.—VOL. XCIV.　　　SATURDAY, JUNE 22, 1889.　　　TWO WHOLE SHEETS} SIXPENCE. By Post, 6½d.

1. Sir George Chetwynd, Bart. 2. The Earl of Durham. 3. Right Hon. James Lowther, Prince Soltykoff, and Earl of March, Arbitrators. 4. Mr. C. Matthews. 5. Sir Charles Russell, Q.C., M.P. 6. Sir Henry James, Q.C., M.P. 7. Mr. Pollard.

THE CHETWYND AND DURHAM TURF LIBEL CASE: SKETCHES IN COURT.

1. Sir George Chetwynd. 2 The Earl of Durham. 3. James Lowther, Prince Soltykoff,
Earl of March, arbitrators. 4. Mr C Matthews. 5. Sir Charles Russell QC MP.
6. Sir Henry James QC MP. 7. Mr Pollard
"The Chetwynd and Durham Turf Libel"
© Illustrated London News Ltd/Mary Evans

CHAPTER EIGHTEEN

Chetwynd v Durham

Charlie pays a high price

On June 10th, 1889 Sir George Chetwynd finally met Lord Durham, not on the beaches of Calais for a duel, but in court number five in the Royal Courts on the Strand.

In April of that year the press reported that Charlie had compromised his own libel action against Durham, with both paying their own costs, and the restoration of his reputation now hung on the outcome of this case. Durham's lawyers strenuously denied that it was a compromise, saying Durham stood by his allegations. A statement that drove Charlie, who had been refused his licence to ride again that year, to write to the press:

> "Mr. George Lewis, Lord Durham's solicitor, knows very well that if the charges Lord Durham made against me could have been proved I should have had to pay Lord Durham's costs of the action as well as my own, and as my solicitor informs me that his costs will exceed £2000 [£252,000], I suppose Lord Durham's costs will amount to a similar sum. I have always been ready and willing to try the question whether I pulled the horses Lord Durham says I pulled; but Lord Durham would not meet me on that question alone, and insisted upon giving evidence about my reputation, as was done in my action against Cox, and I could not fight all the world on that question at a cost of from £200 to £300 a day.

I did not make my reputation, as I was never in my life before charged with any dishonest act, and no single owner of horses has ever complained to the stewards of the way I have ridden. So my reputation must have been made by my enemies."[92]

The hearing of Chetwynd's case against Durham lasted 12 days, partly because the arbitrators did not sit in Ascot week so they all could go racing. Charlie appeared as a witness in support of Chetwynd and as the case progressed it became clear that he was one of the main targets.

Durham's legal team, which had already had one go at him, now had the luxury of a second bite. Their advantage this time, which they would use to full effect, was that Charlie was neither plaintiff nor defendant. As such he did not have a Queen's Counsel acting for him, and was not able to call witnesses to refute the rumours and allegations Durham's legal team and witnesses would fire at him during the hearing.

This time there was no judge and, in particular, no jury of 'tradesmen'. The Jockey Club members had successfully manoeuvred Chetwynd into agreeing that the dispute should be arbitrated before racing experts – a hearing of Chetwynd's dispute with Durham by their peers.

However, when it came down to it, most of his peers found a multitude of reasons not to take on the job. After more than 40 had declined to sit in judgement, the Jockey Club, including the Prince of Wales, had met at the Duke of Richmond's Belgravia house on June 1st, 1889 to try to reach a resolution on the way forward.

---

[92]

Birmingham Daily Gazette, 4th April, 1889

The first decision was to ask Chetwynd and Durham to withdraw the resignations they had both submitted. The second was to appoint the three stewards of the club as the arbitrators. The senior steward, James Lowther MP, a former Cabinet Chief and Chief Secretary for Ireland, said, while they were reluctant to take on the role as it could compromise their position as the club's executive, it was their duty to sacrifice the very strong personal objections they had to being drawn into the matter if they could be the means of "extricating the club from a difficulty."

The arbitrators alone would determine the procedures to be followed and there would also be no appeal from their decision.

Everyone conveniently ignored the fact that Lowther had made a speech in support of Durham's attack on Chetwynd on that fateful evening in 1887 at the Gimcrack Club dinner.

On the allotted Monday in June the parties duly met at the Royal Courts. The Jockey Club had agreed to pay £1 a day for the hire of the courtroom, although the electricity had been turned off for the holiday and the packed court had to be lit by a dozen tall candles. Lowther was joined by his fellow stewards, the Earl of March and Prince Soltykoff, and the three settled down for the duration of the arbitration on the judge's bench.

The next day it transpired that they had put the case in immediate jeopardy. An indignant Lord Chief Justice, after hearing where the stewards had sat, telegraphed the superintendent to forbid the further use of the court.

"Explanations and apologies were, however, offered, and, at the eleventh hour Lord Coleridge telegraphed his permission for the use of the court, on condition the Arbitrators did not sit upon the Judicial Bench."[93]

---

[93] St James's Gazette, 12th June, 1889

It was rumoured that the root of his indignation lay in the fact that stewards had committed the *faux pas* of lunching and smoking in the judges' private rooms.

The case was in many respects a rerun of *Wood v Cox*, with Sir Henry James representing Chetwynd, while Durham had the advantage of Sir Charles Russell's extensive knowledge of racing on his side. The *Northampton Mercury* later commented on the curious lack of dignity about the proceedings, as the arbitrators now sat at the clerk's table below the judge's bench.

> "For want of horse hair, Mr Lowther, Lord March and Prince Soltykoff are just three sporting gentlemen discussing horsey questions across a table with Sir Charles Russell and Sir Henry James."

The prince took very little part in the proceedings and spent most of his time immersed in the racing bible, *Ruff's Guide*.

The case aroused immense interest. It was not often that disputes between a peer of the realm and a baronet over accusations of swindling on the turf were fought out in public. Durham had to prove his main charge, that Chetwynd employed Charlie and trainer Richard Sherrard to 'pull' horses, focusing on Chetwynd's horse Fullerton. Durham's accusation was that the three ran the horse to lose to get a more favourable handicap and longer odds in subsequent races where the horse was ridden to win. He also accused Chetwynd of conniving in malpractices contrary to rules of racing.

Both aristocrats knew they were fighting for their reputations – in those days a precious commodity. The establishment had a ruthless approach to transgressors and, if he lost, Chetwynd would be ostracised by society – "compelled to pay in a currency in which there is no liquidation."[94]

If Durham failed to prove the truth of his charges, he would be seen as having acted in a dangerously impetuous manner, traducing the integrity of racing and another gentleman's honour without just cause.

Chetwynd was already sailing close to the wind so far as Durham was concerned because he made no secret of the fact that his livelihood was openly tied to his racing activities. Durham, who enjoyed the security of £70,000 [£9m] a year from his coal mines alone, had made his views clear in his speech at the Gimcrack Club. To Durham, any member of the aristocracy who used racing to make a living betrayed all that was noble about the sport and their class.

"There is a considerable difference in my mind between winning races and winning money on the turf. The former is a manly, exciting sport of emulation and rivalry, the latter often seen as an ignoble struggle to outwit other people."

His statement conveniently ignored the fact that huge amounts were regularly bet by other members of his class, who often won and lost the equivalent of millions on one race, including those sitting in judgement in the arbitration.

Sir Henry James opened for Chetwynd and did not spare Durham. Chetwynd's betting books and bank statements had been given to Durham's legal team and the Jockey Club back in May 1888. They clearly showed that, in 1887, Chetwynd had backed Fullerton over nine races to the tune of £3,287

---

[94] Lord Reading and his Cases, Derek Walker Smith, 1934

[£425,000]: "Which he lost and paid, and this in races in which Lord Durham said he never backed at all."

The money he won on the horse when it came first brought in £2,190, leaving a net loss in 1887 of £1,097. Yet Durham chose to ignore the evidence and persist with his allegations. When Durham came to give his own evidence, James demanded to know why he had not made more of an inquiry into the facts before making his speech. The evidence to disprove his suspicions was there for all to see in the betting books, which the Jockey Club had had in its possession for over a year.

Chetwynd was first to give evidence. In his memoirs he published the full transcript and the 150 pages show the detailed questioning he had to endure over the running of a large number of horses, a long list of horse purchases and sales and details of bets made and for whom.

He was cross-examined by Sir Charles Russell for five days and, on the fourth day, even the arbitrators expressed a wish that the questioning was brought to a quick conclusion.

George Lambton, Durham's brother, said in his memoir that, while he had never been very intimate with Chetwynd nor ever really liked him:

> "After watching him for days engaged in struggle which practically meant life or death to him, his coolness, his pluck, and the staunch way in which he stuck to his jockey compelled admiration."[95]

In *Old Pink 'un Days*, his reminiscences about writing for the Sporting Times, JB Booth agreed. During a long and searching cross examination, he said Chetwynd was never at a loss to

---

[95] Men and Horses I have Known, George Lambton, 1924

account for his actions as he disposed of one allegation after another.

> "How many men of business in the City of London would have passed through such an ordeal as Sir George Chetwynd has done with so much credit. I do not think there are many who would care to have every action of their career, and every document connected therewith, brought into the fierce light that beats upon the witness-box during a cross-examination by Sir Charles Russell."

James initially focused on the allegation that Fullerton had run inconsistently and when he won, his owner won a lot. When he lost, he lost very little.

Chetwynd's betting book showed the accusation to be false. Chetwynd had also been open about the fact that he bet for Charlie and had given his jockey a share in bets he made but only on his horses when Charlie rode them. He made no secret of having given Charlie this interest in his races and had told the stewards of the Jockey Club that he did so. He might have betted for his jockey once or twice when he was not riding, but he never made a bet for him that would give the jockey an interest in throwing any race he rode in.

Chetwynd made it clear that he had full confidence in Charlie's integrity and had no knowledge of any act being done by the jockey to deceive either himself or anybody else.

Russell then stood to cross-examine. He started in the same way he had finished the defence case in *Wood v Cox*, by asserting that Charlie had a bad reputation and seeking to damn Chetwynd through association: "Is it not a fact that all the witnesses called in the case of *Wood v Cox* gave Wood an evil character?"

James protested against this line of cross-examination but Russell argued it was necessary in order to justify the expression "inexplicable in-and-out running." James said Russell could not be serious in his proposition to which Russell replied: "I am perfectly serious." Lowther decided that as, during his examination-in-chief, James had dwelt upon the good opinion entertained of Charlie in certain quarters, Russell was entitled to deal with the matter without going into detail. Russell said that was all he wanted.

Chetwynd replied that all sorts of rumours flew about in racing. Five years ago everyone was saying there was a jockey ring, but he was positive it never existed. A great many jockeys were suspected, including Fred Archer and Charlie. He also thought it was a good thing for jockeys to bet. He amused the spectators by saying that, if every jockey had money on his mount, it would be a good thing for the owners. At no time had Charlie's riding of his horses induced him to regard him with suspicion and he had never heard it suggested that Charlie was receiving money from owners whose horses he was not riding in a race.

Later in the hearing James secured an important point on behalf of Chetwynd in his cross-examination of Major Egerton, the official handicapper. Egerton confirmed that Chetwynd had told him Fullerton was not fit at the time of his early races and the horse's running could not be taken as an exact index of his proper form; an action Major Egerton described as "very proper."

Jockey Sydney Howard, who would claim he had instructions from Charlie and Richard Sherrard not to exert himself in certain races, also admitted under cross-examination that he had never had such instructions from Chetwynd, nor had he communicated them to Chetwynd.

In his memoirs, Chetwynd said the suspicion that Durham:

"Had the temerity to promulgate was with reference to my horse Fullerton. Very soon his Lordship and his advisers found out what was unfortunately the state of the case – that so far from Fullerton having been a source of profit to me, he had been a most disappointing animal and the occasion of considerable loss, and this charge having broken down they searched vaguely about for mud to fling in the hope some of it might stick."

The mud Durham and his team started to fling focused on Chetwynd's relationship with Charlie. It was clear through both libel hearings that one of Durham's increasingly obsessive concerns was how the relationship between master and servant was being turned on its head in racing, a concern echoed by his QC.

In one exchange Russell questioned Chetwynd on his instructions to Charlie on the riding of Fullerton. He asked: "Did you not give him orders to get off well in front?" Chetwynd replied: "I suggested those orders to him." Which brought the quick response from the leading QC: "A master does not suggest orders; a master gives his servant orders."

Russell then focused on how the two men purchased horses between them. Chetwynd said he had bought a horse called Zadig – at least Charlie had bought it – and had sold it to him. He had not paid for it there and then as Charlie said: "Let it stand over. Pay Sherrard first." The horse was paid for later. Chetwynd said he did not think these pecuniary transactions lessened his authority as master over Charlie.

"Russell: Rather difficult I should think. And you do not consider that in accepting pecuniary assistance from Wood you were doing anything that an ex-

Steward and present member of the Jockey Club ought
not to have done?
Chetwynd: Certainly not. He had never heard it
suggested that Wood was the real master. He was
innocent, and would not accept any insinuation."[96]

Durham's legal team knew that the charge of 'improper
conduct' relied on attacking his jockey and his trainer, Richard
Sherrard. As a result, as the hearing continued, instead of
standing as witnesses to Chetwynd's good conduct, they found
themselves subject to a detailed interrogation on their own
dealings. To the point where it seemed as if bringing them down
was the main objective of the hearing. It left both men
completely exposed as they were unprepared, not represented by
their own counsel and could do little to counter the accusations,
except deny them.

Since Charlie's libel case Durham's team had been digging
for information on all three of their targets, including employing
private detectives, and when Sherrard stood to give evidence they
were soon on notice that their relationship was going to be picked
over in detail. While the trainer was barely audible and
unprepared for the hostile attack, Charlie stood up reasonably
well under the barrage.

Durham's team had to prove Fullerton had been pulled and
the key evidence was due to be given by Sherrard's stable jockey,
Sydney Howard.

The jockey rode the horse at Goodwood and claimed he had
been told not to win. In the witness box Sherrard said, if he gave
Howard any orders at Goodwood, it was to jump off. The
allegation that he had had a conversation with Charlie and
Howard in which the jockey was told to lose the start and drop

---

[96] St James's Gazette, June 12th, 1889

Fullerton out of the race was a vile invention and he only knew one man capable of hatching such a lie – the Newmarket publican Mr Riley.

Sherrard said he had heard that his young jockey was getting into bad company and revealing stable information. He had become the dupe of Riley, who Sherrard knew regularly boasted that he would ruin him as a trainer: "There is not an atom of truth in Howard's statement. Most emphatically I swear it is untrue."[97]

The next witness was Charlie. Russell was about to have a second bite at the man he had failed to prove his case against in *Wood v Cox*. The rules of evidence had done little to protect Charlie from rumours and unproven allegations last time, but this time he did not even have that protection.

He found himself under a sustained attack from Durham's team, who had come armed with evidence of payments, especially between the trainer and the jockey, that they said required detailed explanation.

The relationship between the two was clearly close and complex, with bets being made, horses bought and sold, rents paid and money lent and repaid. Charlie let Chetwynd House to the trainer and said he helped Sherrard "because he wished him well." He had even bred a colt and made present of it to the trainer. The trainer said Charlie had given him several horses and he made the spectators laugh when he said Charlie "was a very liberal fellow".

Charlie admitted that he had also lent Chetwynd money. Russell received short shrift when he questioned why he had not asked Chetwynd the reason for borrowing the money.

---

[97] St James's Gazette, June 15th, 1889

"Well, supposing you were to come to me and ask me to lend you a hundred or two, I shouldn't ask you what you wanted it for but just give you a cheque."[98]

Before proceeding with his cross-examination, Russell requested Charlie's betting books for 1885, 1886 and 1887. Charlie said he had destroyed them – when they were full he always destroyed them. This left him exposed, as he could produce no evidence to counter the many allegations that would now be put to him, except to simply deny them and say he could not explain some figures as it was so long ago. He held up well under the pressure, and at one point, when being questioned on the detail of a transaction caused great laughter by saying: "There you are again, Sir Charles; there you are again."

However, Charlie was vulnerable on the issue of owning horses in breach of the rules. When the attack on him had first started back in 1887 the rule on owning horses had often been ignored and jockeys had not risked losing their licence if found to be the true owner of a horse. That changed with Durham's Gimcrack speech in December 1887, where he announced that, if ownership in breach of the rules was proved in future, jockeys should expect to lose their licence.

The rule would then be applied with ruthless, retrospective ferocity to keep Charlie out of racing for nearly a decade.

Durham's team had dug out evidence that appeared to show Charlie owned horses run in the names of others, and the *St James Gazette* published the cross examination in full where he made an admission in relation to one horse, Jezreel.

Throughout the whole case, the only damaging revelation was over the ownership of Jezreel and Doncaster Cup, which Charlie admitted he had at least part-owned. Jezreel was trained by Howard Macksey.

---

[98] St James's Gazette, June 15th, 1889

Our Honest Charlie Wood

"Wood: He had a slight interest in a horse named Jezreel with Macksey. Jezreel belonged to him and was trained in Macksey's stable. He paid £200 for the horse. Doncaster Cup and Jezreel were the only two horses in training in which he had interest in 1885.

Russell: Will you swear that?

Wood: I can't tell unless I look it up.

Lowther: Come, come, Wood, you have had ample time to look this up. It is a very serious matter.

Russell: I suggest that the alleged sale of the horses Arbaces, Columbine and others was not a genuine or real sale.

Wood: I had no interest in any horses in Sherrard's stable.

Russell: In *Wood v Cox* you swore that you were not interested in any horse which ran in anybody else's name during the last few years. That was not true?

Wood: No. If I said that, it was not true. *(Sensation.)*"[99]

Russell then focused on casting suspicion on Charlie's wealth. Charlie was quite candid over his sources of income: "I made a big income in fees and presents. The Duchess of Montrose and others were very liberal, and I once got £1,000 from Lord Alington. I have invested my savings well, and I have property in Newmarket."

When questioned from whom he had bought his two Newmarket pubs, he amused the spectators by replying that one was bought from James Lowther, now sitting in judgement.

At one point during the trial, Charlie suffered severely from the heat in the courtroom and was reportedly seized with a sudden illness, exhibiting visible symptoms of fever. That illness, in the minds of the press, soon turned into a false report that he

---

[99] St James's Gazette, June 17th, 1889

had committed suicide by jumping from the East Cliff at Ramsgate.

"A few days back, whilst in attendance at the Law Courts in connection with the Chetwynd-Durham turf scandal, he was obliged to retire to his home at Brighton, through indisposition, and the immense amount of worry and the great mental strain that he has undergone in the law cases, has, it is asserted, made him very low spirited and dejected...

Following so closely the death of the late Fred Archer, such a tragic end is much to be lamented, and much sympathy is expressed for his widow."[100]

As the case proceeded, much as in *Wood v Cox*, it became clear that Durham was on a crusade and was not particularly concerned by the lack of solid evidence. He was out to attack the reputations of as many people as possible in the hope it would scare everyone else into line.

During his own evidence he introduced so many fresh names in distinctly unflattering terms, that the arbitrators found themselves bombarded by indignant letters and telegrams. They were forced to say that anyone whose reputation had been impugned could come and defend themselves if they wished.[101]

During his cross examination Durham also entered into some sharp passages with James that served to highlight him as a man accustomed to having his own way, and angry to find himself confined to the points raised by the clever and hostile QC, a man he disliked intensely.

---

[100] Derby Daily Telegraph, July 17th, 1889
[101] The Mayfair Calendar, Horace Wyndham, 1925

It was clear from his final speech that Russell knew he had failed to prove the charges of pulling horses; the best he could manage was to assert that Chetwynd must have known something was not right. He made racing pay, to the tune of £5,000 or £6,000 [£630,000 to £750,000] a year and he was so involved with Charlie and Sherrard that he could not disclaim their conduct.

Russell's difficulty was that, in the absence of any proof, he had to depend almost entirely on asserting that Chetwynd must have known because there were circumstances that might reasonably have led him to suspect wrong doing.

Sir Henry James was having none of it. In his impassioned final speech, which took over five hours, he dismissed Durham's case as a house of cards built on suspicion alone.

No man, not even Durham, had a right to become a speculator in slander. He had relied entirely on rumour and suspicion when he made his speech at York. As Francis Bacon had said over 300 years before: "There is nothing which makes a man suspect much more than knowing little." Durham knew little and suspected much. He made no attempt to establish the facts and his Gimcrack speech was a deliberate and acrimonious attack on Chetwynd. Chetwynd should not be found guilty just because Durham had a desire to do good.

James said he had embarked on a campaign with no better arms than a plentiful stock of suspicion and the *Racing Calendar*. He did not question the motive, but good results must not be achieved by bad means. The mistake Durham made was in assuming the dishonesty and deducing the dishonesty from the assumption. He knew nothing of the variation in the form of the horses and the particular way they ran on various courses. He knew nothing of the conditions likely to affect Chetwynd's judgement in backing horses.

He accused him simply because he was Sir George Chetwynd and "stuck up for Wood."

There was no calling, he said, to which false rumour was more likely to attach itself than the calling of a jockey. A disappointed gambler was much more likely to blame the jockey than the owner or trainer. But rumour is not truth. Until his banishment, Charlie was "employed by men as honourable as any who had ever lived."

Chetwynd placed bets for Charlie on horses that he was riding, which it was common practice. Jockeys also regularly bet on races. Fred Archer, up until his death 18 months before, had been famous for his betting. Chetwynd had borrowed money from Charlie. That was not a crime either, although Durham clearly thought it was wrong that a servant was wealthy enough to lend money to his master.

Many distinguished owners also employed Charlie, but Durham had not said to them: "You ought to have known about these things, because I knew."

Durham's counsel had attempted to make capital out of the fact that Chetwynd had confidence in Charlie, but he shared that confidence with General Williams, the Duke of Beaufort and the Duke of Portland. After the result in *Wood v Cox* it was not for him to say he believed Charlie guilty of charges that had not been proved against him. James concluded his speech with:

> "An eloquent appeal to the arbitrators to pause before they condemned a fellow-man to pass the rest of his life in ignominy, and expressed his confident opinion that Sir George Chetwynd would walk from that court into the light of day with no man to shun him and no man to condemn him of having done anything

unbecoming a gentleman of honour. *(Applause, which was suppressed.)*"[102]

The arbitrators did not have to sum up before closing the case and everyone went home to await their decision. When it came on June 30th, it was delivered as a bare announcement, without explanation. In the end they sat firmly on the fence, finding for Chetwynd on the more serious charge of 'pulling' horses and awarding him a farthing damages, but finding the charge of lesser malpractices proved.

The *Sporting Times*, reflecting on the case in 1924, said that result was most unsatisfactory for everyone concerned as the arbitrators' main objective seemed to be to whitewash both Chetwynd and Durham:

"Thus the verdict – farthing damages – did not satisfy wounded vanity, even if it did prove that Lord Durham had failed to substantiate his charges."

Until his dying day, Durham believed racing should remain the preserve of the wealthy aristocracy, men who were independently wealthy and could afford to lose money. In his one-man crusade to cleanse the Augean stables of those he despised for doing well out of racing, he was found to have stated more than he could prove and ended up paying his own substantial costs.[103]

His actions divided the racing community and an attempt to raise money to help him meet the cost of defending William Cox and himself only raised £329 after a year. Durham had declined to accept the money and donated it to a benevolent fund for trainers and jockeys.

[102] St James's Gazette, June 28th, 1889
[103] The Saturday Review, July 6th, 1889

Although the decision was essentially a draw, Chetwynd was the loser for, like Charlie before him, the damages awarded were a contemptuous sum, suggesting his poor reputation did not entitle him to more. This, coupled with the fact that the other part of the decision – even though it was more a general allegation – had gone against him, was enough to destroy his reputation.

"It was on a Saturday afternoon at Alexandra Park when [Sir George] received the news of the Arbitrators' award in his action against Lord Durham. It was a hot day, but he looked delightfully cool in his suit of flannels and a straw hat with a coloured band. Someone handed him a telegram. 'One farthing damages' was the message. 'Rather short odds' he said quietly. It must have been a terrific blow to him as he had been grossly libelled and grievously wronged. He fully expected the verdict with substantial damages, but he did not whine or find fault with the judges. He had always taken Fortune's rewards and buffets with equal calm, and no one who watched him for the rest of the afternoon would have imagined that he had experienced the greatest blow of his life."[104]

Chetwynd, Charlie and Sherrard stood as the scapegoats for their three professions: owner, jockey and trainer. Charlie went into the trial without his licence to ride. After the grilling he sustained on the ownership of horses and his admission, he emerged to find the Jockey Club about to warn him and the trainer Henry Macksey off Newmarket Heath and all premises owned by the Jockey Club. Richard Sherrard was told he could continue to train, but not in Newmarket.

---

[104] The Old Pink 'un Days, JB Booth, 1924

JB Booth, in the *Old Pink 'un Days*, was unimpressed:

> "Charley Wood... came well out of the trials, so far as his character for honesty and straight riding was concerned, but it was proved that he had transgressed against the rules of the Jockey Club by betting and owning horses, two things which, one is carefully assured, are unknown to the present race of riders. It was for these offences that he was punished and not for 'pulling' or 'squaring'. Wood had to run the course twice, having been severely cross examined during his own action against Cox, but he made no slips in his evidence."[105]

The arbitrators' decision left Chetwynd between a rock and a hard place. His first step was to see if he could appeal, but he had accepted before the arbitration that there was no right of appeal. So he took the only course open to him and wrote to the Jockey Club offering to resign.

> "Having accepted the Stewards as the tribunal to judge me, I am aware that from their recorded judgement I have no appeal in law.... Of the original charge, always the main one, made by Lord Durham I am entirely acquitted. To which of the lesser charges the judgement of the arbitrators extends I know not, and I presume no member of the club, except the Stewards, does know. Still, having been a party to some breaches of the rules of racing, I am, by the judgement given, condemned."[106]

---

[105] The Old Pink 'un Days, JB Booth, 1924
[106] St James's Gazette, July 8th, 1889

He said he tendered his offer to resign in the full reliance that: "The great majority of the club will be just, I need not say generous, enough to believe that my resignation involves no admission on my part of the correctness of the award given." Chetwynd's son, Guy, later said his father resigned in the belief that Durham would do the same. When Durham did not, his father came to view his resignation as the worst mistake of his life.

While they accepted his resignation, he received no direct sanction from the Jockey Club. He was not barred from any premises and could continue to own and race horses. The *St James Gazette* took the view that this was partly because he has been punished enough, but also because it was known that many other persons in an equally high position were similar offenders against the rules of racing.

In his memoir *Men and Horses I have Known*, George Lambton claimed his brother, Durham, was not a vindictive man. He recounted an incident when Leopold Rothschild asked if he thought it was possible to bring about a reconciliation between Chetwynd and Durham, as he knew that Chetwynd was anxious for it:

> "My brother, who is the quickest of men to relent when the fight over, at once agreed to a meeting, which took place at Newmarket."

This was not the view taken by Chetwynd, however. In his memoir, *Racing Reminiscences*, he recounts an episode that showed the vindictiveness with which Durham continued to pursue his target.

A month after the decision, he said, Sir Frederick Johnstone had a "little passage of arms of his own" with Durham at

Sandown Park. Chetwynd was in the Jockey Club stand, and Durham asked Johnstone what right he had to be there. "If you mean that you want me to turn George Chetwynd out of this stand I'll see you damned first!" was the curt reply.

The arbitration, far more than the libel trial he brought against William Cox, severely damaged Charlie. He had no redress. His only course was to assert, with some justification, that he was no better or worse than many of his contemporaries.

His term of punishment would be severe.

CHAPTER NINETEEN

Derby Day, 1897

No horse ever galloped down from Tattenham Corner in more exquisite fashion

Early in the straight, with the finishing post now in sight, Galtee More and Velasquez increase their speed and move past the other horses. Barring an injury at full gallop, the race is now between just them.

COACHES AT THE WINNING POST.

"Coaches at the Winning Post"
The Illustrated Sporting and Dramatic News, 1897
© Illustrated London News Ltd/Mary Evans

Charlie can feel his blood quickening. The magnificent colt beneath him does not feel tired, does not need coaxing to race beyond his capabilities. Galtee More is still full of running, and far from not coming down the hill well, Charlie knows that none of the horses he has ridden before in the Derby had ever galloped down from Tattenham Corner in more exquisite fashion.

As the battle is joined between the two Charlie moves Galtee More once more to the inside and takes up the running.

This is the point of greatest danger. His horse has plenty more to give. But is Jack Watts feeling the same on Valasquez?

Every jockey knows never to turn his head to look at the other runners as the finishing post draws near. Vital seconds can be lost. But as Charlie draws ahead he cannot stop himself glancing at the horse and rider galloping beside him.

At that moment, he sees Jack Watts start to urge Velasquez to make one last effort. His mount answers with a surge of power, bringing them back level with Galtee More.

The excitable crowd see the move and the shout goes up: the favourite is beaten.

CHAPTER TWENTY

A Cruel Exile

Into the wilderness

On July 18th, 1889, a month after the *Chetwynd v Durham* case finished, the second deadly blow fell when the *Racing Calendar* announced:

> "The Stewards of the Jockey Club have warned Charles Wood off the Racecourse and Heath at Newmarket, and off all other premises belonging to the Jockey Club... The Stewards of the Jockey Club have withdrawn RG Sherrard's licence to train at Newmarket."

Charlie had been exiled and it was rumoured that the Jockey Club's intention was to never let him ride in a race again. They might be persuaded to allow him back onto their racecourses and Newmarket Heath and allow him to train, so long as he never applied for a licence to ride.

If that had been the intention, they severely underestimated their man and his deep sense of injustice. Those that knew him well knew he was driven by a determination to clear his name; and the best way to do that was on the back of a racehorse.

With Charlie's removal, there was a dearth of riders about Charlie's old weight and trainers and owners were finding it difficult coming to terms with losing the services of the country's leading jockey. Sir Francis Lawley wrote: "With nearly 50 years of experience of horse racing in all its phases, Mathew Dawson lately told a friend of mine that Wood is at this moment the best jockey in England, one who never loses his head, or is in too great a hurry, or abuses his horses, and that the Turf is a loser by the suspension of his licence."[107]

It also came as no surprise to the racing community that Durham and the Jockey Club continued to be troubled by 'in-and-out' performances.

Charlie applied to get his licence back in 1890. He was refused. He tried again in 1891, 1892, 1893, 1894, 1895 and 1896. Every year the Jockey Club refused him. Each year the press clamour over the injustice grew.

After the full ban was imposed, Charlie put all his brood mares and racehorses up for sale. It took place at Newmarket, on July 9th, 1889 and was a well-attended event. After the sale he moved to Essex and started living the life of a country gentleman at Little Waltham Hall, Chelmsford. For solace he turned to his second love, hunting, and on Saturday November 30th, 1889 he was seen out with the Essex Hounds, which had met at the King William Inn in Harlow. It was a lifestyle he continued when he took his family to stay at his house in Brighton, and it helped to keep him riding fit as he waited for his licence. He later moved to Hailsham in East Sussex and set himself up with a large household and started hunting with the Eastbourne Foxhounds.

The *Sporting Sketch* reported that life was treating him well.

"For a man who has taken care of himself as he has done, he is still in the prime of his life. His hunting has helped to keep him fit. He [provided a horse for] a friend of mine one day with the Eastbourne Foxhounds, and on my asking my friend afterwards how he had been carried, he said: 'Never better; no man could wish to ride a more magnificent hunter.'"

---

[107] The Bench and the Jockey Club, Sir Francis Lawley, 1889

It was perhaps unfortunate that Durham served as a Jockey Club steward from 1891 to 1894, and it was only as his persecutor's term ended that Charlie started to be allowed back. After serving seven years of suspension, the first indication that the intense pressure to reinstate him was starting to bear fruit came on November 1st, 1894 with the short announcement:

> "The Stewards of the Jockey Club have withdrawn the notice published on July 18th 1889, warning Charles Wood off the racecourse and Heath at Newmarket."

Charlie could train horses, attend races and ride trials. Bendingo, in the *Penny Illustrated* was delighted.

> "I am glad to find Charles Wood's term of punishment ended. Whether [he] was guilty or not guilty when tried by the law courts and the Jockey Club does not count now. What the betting public knows is that Charles Wood was found guilty of breaking the Jockey Club's rules and on that count most severely punished. After him came a whole row of jockeys who were also found guilty by the Jockey Club, and, having suffered a moderate term of warning off, were let back. As those were restored to their friends and relations, the question arose, why would he be left out."

But he still could not ride in a race and the rumours started that he had passed the point where age and fitness would allow him to race, even if he got his licence back. The *Sheffield Independent* on November 7th, 1894 reported that John Corlett of the *Sporting Times* was saying that Charlie has no desire to ride races. It was outraged at the destruction of his career: "The punishment that was meted out to him was very severe, seeing that all was ever proved against him was that he was half owner of a horse that ran in the name of some other person."

Corlett may have been throwing up a smokescreen to try lull the Jockey Club into thinking they could give him back his licence as he would not race again.

The public demand for his return continued and the steady stream of letters to the papers calling on the stewards of the Jockey Club to restore his licence did not abate. In May 1895 there were widespread reports of a petition being presented to the Jockey Club demanding his licence was reinstated. The move followed a report in the *Sheffield Independent* on April 29th, 1895 highlighting the fact that Charlie had been banished for seven years and:

> "Considering the payments now made to jockeys of the first rank, Wood's loss of income must have cost him... £50,000 [£6.3m]. When, says Mr John Corlett, a sort of amnesty was declared not long ago, it is to be regretted that Wood was not included in it, as he was the one against whom the least was proved, and his punishment was the greatest. With the punishment made excessive, sympathy is apt to run round to the punished, and that at all times is a thing to be guarded against."

Powerful voices within the Jockey Club were also at work on Charlie's behalf. Lord Rosebery made it public that he wanted Charlie to ride his horse, Sir Visto, in that year's Derby.[108] All to no avail.

However, in 1896, the Jockey Club was clearly starting to feel the pressure. It announced that it would bring the question of his jockey's licence before the club when it assembled during a race

[108] A Pink 'un Remembers, JB Booth, 1937

meeting at Newmarket in March: "in order that they may elicit the general opinion of members thereupon before deciding what course to adopt."

Clearly the opinions were not favourable as his licence was again refused. The expectation that he would be reinstated had taken such a hold that the Jockey Club's refusal took everyone by surprise. On April 10th, 1886 the *Sportsman* said it regretted that the stewards did not consider that Charlie's suspension for eight years and consequent loss of the opportunity of earning a very big annual income was sufficient punishment. But, as the meetings were all held behind closed doors, the paper could only assume the Jockey Club had "facts unknown to the world at large" for continuing to banish him. It speculated that the refusal probably meant that Charlie's sentence was for life.

However, during 1896, several owners continued to make it clear they were increasingly frustrated by the Jockey Club's intransigence. US owner Richard Croker was desperate for Charlie's return. His horse, Americus Ray, was favourite at Kempton Park Jubilee Stakes on May 9th, 1896.

"Mr Croker will be sorely disappointed in the action of the stewards of the Jockey Club, which after a lengthy deliberation has refused to grant a jockey's licence to Charles Wood, one of the most popular and capable jockeys that ever rode in England. Wood has not been able to get a licence since 1887, in which year he finished up at the head of the list of winning jockeys. Mr Croker had expected to secure his services to ride Americus in the Jubilee Stakes and Montauk in the Derby. He will now probably have to rely on Clayton, who is a jockey of only moderate ability."[109]

---

[109] The New York Times, April 22nd, 1896

While the clamour grew for his full return, Charlie was preparing for his family's future. He bought the estate village of Jevington, near Eastbourne from the Duke of Devonshire in November 1896. It included most of the houses in the small downland village and a farm of 1,000 acres.

CHAPTER TWENTY ONE

Derby Day, 1897

Charles Wood has not been seen to greater advantage

Charlie has seen Jack Watts urging Velasquez to make one last effort. The crowd has seen Velasquez surge forward and draw level. They start to anticipate an upset.

But Charlie knows his horse has much more to give. He asks Galtee More to fully extend himself for the first time and feels the surge of power beneath him as the colt answers his urging.

THE FINISH.

"The Finish"
The Illustrated Sporting and Dramatic News, 1897
© Illustrated London News Ltd/Mary Evans

A roar of delight goes up when the crowd see the favourite is now half a length in front.

Judge Robinson waits at the finish, amid an excited crowd of spectators pushing and shoving to get the best view, leaning into the course to try to see the galloping horses bearing down on them.

Their first clear sight, as the lead horses approach, is of a crimson cap. Charlie Wood and Galtee More are in the lead. With each stride, Velasquez's chances of making up the distance once more and overtaking Galtee More diminish.

As they race past the post, Galtee More is still full of running, with his ears pricked. Charlie allows himself a second look back at Jack Watts on Velasquez.

He takes a moment to absorb what he sees – it is a fact – he has beaten Velasquez into second place by a good two lengths.

He has won the Jubilee Derby and his heart is fit to burst. His friends and family, all those who had never lost their belief in him through his long ordeal, are waiting at the winner's enclosure to join him in his moment of triumph, his moment of redemption.

When the race is over, everyone says an easier victory has not been witnessed for many years and Charlie has not been seen to greater advantage at any time during his professional career. All the way through he had Galtee More well in hand and he won in beautiful style.

Before he can start to celebrate, he has to pull the colt up. But Galtee More is enjoying himself so much he has no desire to stop and gallops all the way back to the paddock.

CHAPTER TWENTY TWO

Triumphant Return

More sinned against that sinning

The Jockey Club finally relented as the 1897 racing season loomed. On January 22ⁿᵈ, 1897 the *Daily News* announced that Charlie Wood's name had appeared in the list of jockeys being given licences to ride for that season.

> "This will be a most popular decision as the racing public has long since decided that that this jockey has been sufficiently punished and that the time for his reinstatement has arrived."[110]

Presented to Charlie by Martin Rucker and his wife to commemorate
Charlie's win on Northallerton at Liverpool on March 27ᵗʰ 1897

---

[110] Daily News, January 22nd, 1897

The Jockey Club may have hoped that they had delayed his reinstatement long enough to force him to retire. However, they had severely underestimated his determination to pick up and carry on where he had left off.

He wanted to clear his name, and the best way he knew to achieve that was to prove he was as good a jockey as he had been before the ban. He was fit and confident that he retained all his old nerve and dash.

In a letter to the press he thanked his many friends for their congratulations. He said they were too numerous to reply to personally, as he had received upwards of 600 friendly letters and telegrams. His reappearance soon showed any doubters that he was a man of strong will and great determination of character.

"He possesses the ability to conquer difficulties that to some would appear crushing. For a man of [42] to begin race riding again after so long a period of retirement is truly remarkable; it shows what care "Charlie" has taken of himself during the past ten years. He resided in a large country house at Hailsham, near Eastbourne, for some time, and made himself very popular in the district. He kept several hunters, and was an enthusiastic follower of the local foxhounds. That is how he has maintained his condition and 'fitness.'"[111]

Charlie quickly set about re-establishing himself at Newmarket. In February, the Press Association's Newmarket correspondent reported on his arrival back at Lowther House.

"He made an early start today at his old profession, doing some hard gallops on several two-year-olds and

---

[111] Sporting Sketch, March 31st, 1897

old horses on Water Hall Ground. He averred that, from the time of his first mounting, he felt in every way up to his old form, and was never in better health. He gave it to be understood Lord Rosebery and Mr Martin Rucker will be the first to require his services, and said that, all being well, he will make a start at Lincoln. Wood is delighted with the cordial reception which he has met with since his return to the saddle."[112]

One of the first trainers to beat a path to his door was Sam Darling, eager to book him to ride Galtee More for all of his races that season, including the 2,000 Guineas, Derby and St Leger. Charlie must have been delighted with that meeting. At this point in his career, he had not won the Guineas or the St Leger, and Galtee More gave every indication of being a great horse.

His debut took place at the season opener at Lincoln in March and a record crowd greeted him with standing ovations. The *Sporting Sketch* reported on Lincoln, saying that a pleasant feature of the opening day was his return to active service.

"The popular feeling was emphasised by the enthusiastic greeting which was extended to him as he wended his way quietly across from the weighing room to the paddock, and prepared to have the leg up on his first mount. For weeks past the famous middle weight has been working very hard at riding exercise, his name being seldom missing when trials were on the tapis, and as a natural result he stripped as fit as a fiddle, and was able to ride at the nice weight of 7st 11lb, though the

---

[112] Yorkshire Evening Post, February 9th, 1897

wasp like dimensions of his waist were suggestive of but a very light breakfast, if, indeed, he had indulged at all in that very necessary meal."[113]

His first race confirmed that he had lost none of his old skill. He rode El Diablo in the Lincoln Trial Stakes to a dead heat with Sam Loates on Overdue, which counted as a win. The large crowd cheered him to the start, and gave him a standing ovation as he returned to the scales to weigh-in. In 1935 Charlie still held fond memories of the moment, including Lord Durham's offer to provide his first ride. He told the *Coventry Evening Telegraph*:

> "The first race I rode in after my return to the saddle... was a dead heat at Lincoln. Lord Durham had offered to enter a horse, especially so that I could have my first ride after any return, for him. He thought it would do me good if he did this, but I was unable to accept. I had fixed up with Lord Rosebery, for a retainer of £2,000 a year, and I had £1,500 a year for a second claim."[114]

He was back, and back in style. The *Sporting Sketch* was full of admiration saying that his case in some respects mirrored that of George Fordham. Both resumed their profession when no longer in their first youth; both were acknowledged to be very fine jockeys.

> "During the past few weeks – that is, since the inaugural meeting at Lincoln – there have been many interminable conversations amongst racing men as to whether Wood is as good a jockey now as he was 10

---

[113] Sporting Sketch, March 31st, 1897
[114] Coventry Evening Telegraph, November 21st, 1935

years ago. There is no doubt that Wood retains his old dash and nerve, his fine judgement of pace, and quickness at both ends. Those who profess to see deterioration cannot tell us where it is. They are warmest in their criticisms after backing one of his losing mounts. Without for my own past caring to sit in judgement, I feel convinced that in a few short weeks most of us will be singing Wood's praises, and at the end of the season he will have a most satisfactory record. One fact in his favour is that he loves the game. It was not need of money that induced him to begin riding again."[115]

Meanwhile, some commentators were making their condemnation of the Jockey Club's harsh treatment of Charlie very clear, especially overseas. *The Press*, published in New Zealand, did not hold back.

"In congratulating Wood upon the removal of the ban, I can only express surprise that said withdrawal should not have taken place at least four years since. Nine years of enforced inactivity is a terrible punishment for any jockey, especially for one who was practically un-convicted of any offence against turf morality. That Wood has throughout been more sinned against than sinning, I shall always believe... If we were only to credit half the fairy tales that are told of jockeys, not a licence should be renewed from one season to another. In race riding, as in other professions, honesty is not only the best policy, but the most remunerative one; and when it is considered how much easier it is to 'stop' a horse in the stable than on the racecourse, it is

---

[115] Sporting Sketch, March 31st, 1897

disgraceful that open accusations of pulling should be
made against men who are, probably far more
'straight' than their accusers."

The *St Louis Post Dispatch* was also harsh in its criticism. Free
of the conventions of the UK press, it did not pull its punches.
Charlie, it said, had been known worldwide as the only real rival
to Fred Archer. For nine years he has been purging himself of his
offence and, during all that long period, no word of complaint
from him has ever reached the public ear, which the paper
viewed as wise – he took his punishment and had therefore got
his licence back. If he had rebelled he might never have been
reinstated. In the paper's view, Charlie's case was one of the most
infamous in the history of the turf and it did not spare Durham,
feeling free to refer to his divorce case without fear, calling him:

"A purist among purists, so far as turf affairs are
concerned, though a man with an unenviable character
as regards his domestic affairs."

The *Dispatch* reminded its readers that Sir George Chetwynd
was exonerated of all the serious charges made against him and
Charlie won his libel case, although it cost him may thousands to
do so. He had completely refuted the charges but this did not
prevent the stewards of the Jockey Club from taking away his
licence. The paper could only conclude that the passing of time
made it appear more than probable that Charlie had been made
a scapegoat.

Just as Charlie returned to racing in 1897, the style of race
riding was undergoing a radical change with the arrival of
American jockey Tod Sloan. Sloan rode with short stirrups, in the
style now used by all jockeys, although at the start the British

jockeys said he looked like a 'monkey up a stick'. Inevitably, his style was highly controversial when he first arrived, in the same way as Joseph Dawson's radical approach to training horses had been when he arrived in Newmarket in the 1860s. Once Sloan started winning, every jockey started shortening his stirrups. Charlie resisted the change, although he later confessed to shortening his stirrups be a hole or two. He eventually accepted that the new style of riding was permanent:

> "Charlie Wood, the well-known trainer, expresses the opinion that no amount of discussion will alter the present style riding. He believes that, 'like many other things, it has come to stay.'"[116]

Charlie went on to ride 122 winners in 1897 and finish third in the championship. In 1898 he was fourth in the list. In 1899 he was sixth with 90 wins. He kept his weight down, averaging between 7st 12lb and 8st.

He would not be champion jockey again. For the rest of his life he must have been left with the painful thought that, if he had not been banished for nearly a decade, he might have established his place in history as one of the greatest jockeys of all time.

---

[116] Exeter and Plymouth Gazette, January 25th, 1913

DEVONSHIRE HOUSE,'
JEVINGTON.
SUSSEX.

March 16th 1900

dear Sir

In reply to your letter
The races which gave me the
most pleasure ~~took~~ to win were
those in which I won on
Gallée Moore after my return
to the turf namely two Thousand
Derby & St Ledger

Yours truly
C. Wood

AUTOGRAPH LETTER FROM CHARLEY WOOD:
HIS FAVOURITE VICTORIES.

CHAPTER TWENTY THREE

Derby Day, 1897

A huge sea of cheering people

Charlie eventually manages to pull Galtee More back to a walk and they slowly make their way through the cheering crowds to the bear pit in front of the weighing room. The winners' enclosure is so small it is hard to get the first and second horses in, let alone all the owners, jockeys and their supporters. Charlie is right back where he belongs.

> "We ran almost into the Paddock and then returned through a huge sea of cheering people. Mr Gubbins was quickly on the nearside with congratulatory pats for Galtee's neck and my knee… I had won my second Derby, and I tell you, I was the proudest man on the course. I think after my nine years the people were glad to see me win."[117]

John Gubbins takes the lead rein and holds his horse amid vociferous shouting and cheering from the Irish spectators. Charlie weighs in and when the Clerk of the Scales, Mr Manning, pronounces 'all right':

> "The crowd cheered again, more, as it seemed, for the victory of a famous jockey who had been under a cloud than for the horse or his owner, although Mr Gubbins came in for many a hearty congratulation as

---

[117] Pall Mall Gazette, June 5th, 1897

he led Galtee More back to the weighing room door."[118]

The *Sporting Times* agrees: "The cheers of the onlookers… were a good deal for Charlie Wood, whose return to the fullest share of Fortune's favours are much appreciated. Wood has been riding in great form throughout the two days."

Having borne off the prize Galtee More is as calm and as good tempered amid the hubbub as if he has lived all his life in the middle of an excited crowd, including overenthusiastic souvenir hunters. Darling later recalled:

"Many people in the crowd were securing hairs from his tail as he passed along. He went through the ordeal very well, but I was most anxious to get to the paddock as quickly as possible, as otherwise I am sure he would not have had a hair left."[119]

Charlie's friend, the trainer James Ryan, comes up alongside the victorious jockey. The year before Ryan had watched the Prince of Wales's Persimmon win the Derby, standing with Charlie at the rails. As Persimmon passed the post Charlie had heaved a great sigh: "I'd give £1,000 to be back in the saddle again and riding the winner of the Derby!" "I'll remind you of that, Charlie, when you're in the saddle and riding the winner," Ryan had said, "and it won't be long now."

Ryan reaches up with an outstretched hand to a jubilant Charlie: "What did I tell you last year? You didn't believe me, but here you are, and riding the winner – and I don't want your £1,000!"[120]

---

[118] Daily News, June 8th, 1897
[119] Sam Darling's Reminiscences, 1914
[120] Pall Mall Gazette, June 5th, 1897

John Gubbins is also a happy man. His horse will go down in the history books as the first Irish-bred, Irish-owned horse to win the Derby. The rulers of racing not only had to sit and watch the man they thought they had destroyed ride the winner but, in Queen Victoria's Diamond Jubilee year, the winning horse and owner were Irish; with calls for Irish Home Rule gaining momentum and the fight for Irish independence heating up.

Across Ireland the colt's win provokes enthusiastic celebrations, with bonfires lit on the top of the Galtee Mountains to mark the "humiliation of the Saxon." In his biography, *Sam Darling's Reminiscences*, the trainer tells the story of his journey to Ireland after the win. At Limerick station a train porter came up and said: "Shure, are you Mr Sam Darling?" Having established that he was, he went off and soon returned with all the porters. "Your honour, we're delighted to meet you. You trained Galtee More when he won the first English Derby for Ireland, and shure we will never forget the whiskey flying about that night. The mountains were alight with it!"

The politically charged nature of the win was reflected by the *Sportsman* the next day.

"The Irish grumble that we overtax them. The wrong is certainly not aggravated by under-representation. Again, an Irishman is the Lord Chief Justice of England [Sir Charles Russell, who acted for the defence in both the libel cases involving Charlie], another is Commander in Chief of the British Army, they have taken the Diamond Jubilee Derby, and they have been sweeping the board of racing pretty freely this year. Can they with any conscience be dissatisfied longer? If they have not Home Rule, they rule and best us in a good many ways."

The *Globe* added that Irishmen should now thoroughly understand how heartily Englishmen can congratulate their compatriots on the other side of St George's Channel.[121]

The political significance was also recognised in the US, with the *Washington Times* later claiming that: "The sentiment is so strong that if Ireland was a kingdom there is little doubt that Mr Gubbins would be elected to fill the honoured position of King."[122]

The *Sporting Life* congratulated the team behind Galtee More, saying few in a lifetime can expect to breed such a racer as Gubbins had with this colt. Sam Darling had quite excelled himself as a master of the training art, winning three races in six weeks and bringing the colt out in such fine fettle for the Derby, which bespoke patience and skill of the highest order. It added:

"The balance of fate is happily adjusted again in the fact that after Charley Wood's long retirement he should ride the winners of the Guineas, the Derby and in all equine probability, the Leger in the same year."

Booth in his memoir, *The Pink 'un Remembers*, agreed. Charlie had never lost confidence in himself, and now he had his reward.

"There is no need at this day to recall the scandal and the legal action which drove Charles Wood from the Turf, but his behaviour during the long period of suspension earned him respect... During the whole period of his suspension his weight varied but a few ounces, a fact which speaks for the determination and strength of character of a man who saw his livelihood

[121] The Globe, June 3rd, 1897
[122] Washington Times, September 9th, 1897

gone, and his career as a leading jockey of his day, for all he knew, at an end."

It was Charlie's finest hour and one that he savoured for the rest of his life. On March 16th, 1900 he wrote to the *Sketch* from his home in Jevington, Sussex,[123] saying the races which gave him the most pleasure: "Were those in which I won on Galtee More after my return."

The *Sketch* commented: "The letter of the 'The People's Charlie' as Charles Wood is popularly called, speaks for itself, and the torrent of cheering when Galtee More passed the winning post, followed by Valasquez, was pleasing testimony to the jockey's popularity."[124]

He went on to win the St Leger on Galtee More and secured the colt's place in the history books as the first Irish bred, Irish owned winner of the coveted Triple Crown - the 2000 Guineas, the Derby and the St Leger.

Charlie still has one more race to run that day. In the Effingham Plate he enjoyed another win on the second favourite, The Nipper.

---

[123] See page 188
[124] The Sketch, May 30th, 1900

TRAINING ON THE SUSSEX DOWNS—A VISIT TO JEVINGTON

1. Jevington.   2. Mr. C. Wood on the Downs.   3. After the morning's work.   4. Mr. C. Wood's string at cantering exercise.   5. The string passing Friston Windmill.
6. The New Stables—Sirdar (on left), Colonel Wasac (on right).   7. Newtown (on left), Haka (on right).   8. A few of the Boxes at Mr. J. Wood's Stables.

"Training on the Sussex Downs – a visit to Jevington"
The Illustrated Sporting and Dramatic News © Illustrated London News Ltd/Mary
Evans

CHAPTER TWENTY FOUR

To Jevington

"Good things" may be kept quiet enough at Jevington

As an old inhabitant – not quite the oldest but a very reverend seigneur, who was entitled to say something on that account – said, "This is a lovely place for a man to settle down at calmly to spend his declining years, because locally the difference between living and dying is so small that he won't really know when he is gone."[125]

Charlie's plans for the future of his family now start to fall into place. Once he had been allowed back to train in 1894 he had started to look for somewhere he and his son James could train together. After everything that had happened, he had ruled out a permanent return to Newmarket.

Over the years he had got to know East Sussex and the South Downs well. At the height of his career he had had a winter house in Brighton, and after he had been banned, he moved his family to Woodside House, near Hailsham in East Sussex, from where he and Ellen spend much of their time hunting over the downs. He had often ridden for the Duke of Devonshire, who at that time owned vast swathes of the land around Eastbourne, including most of the small village of Jevington, seven miles from Eastbourne, nestled in a valley high on the downs.

Charlie bought the estate village and 1,000 acre farm from Devonshire in late 1896. Jevington was a good choice, as it had long been established as a training centre.

---

[125] Illustrated Sporting and Dramatic News, January 13th, 1900

Charles Wood - Family Archive

"Racehorses seem to have been trained on the Sussex Downs almost from time immemorial, and, as history records, great winners have been sent out from that quarter. It is admirably adapted by Nature for the purpose indicated. Long stretches of galloping ground are available; the air is salubrious; touts are not numerous enough to become objectionable and in summer the 'going' continues to be satisfactory. Jevington is one of the quietest training places in the world. Some distance from a railway station, nestling under the hills in picturesque seclusion, though within easy walking distance of Eastbourne, this little village seems lost in slumberous content. But for the stables it would show few signs of active or sporting enterprise."[126]

With the imminent arrival of Charlie and his family, Jevington started to attract a lot of interest as a training centre. The *Sportsman* sent a correspondent down to investigate.

"Now that the jockey-trainer, Charles Wood, has taken, or is about to take up his training quarters at Jevington, increased attention will be drawn to this quiet village, which lies in sheltered valley beneath the famous South Downs. The old training establishment of Mr William Clay, now presided over by his son and son-in-law, Messrs Arthur Clay and William Viney (the trainers of Euclid when he won the Jubilee Stakes and the Lincoln Handicap), should also come in for larger share of patronage, for two more conscientious and hardworking adepts at their profession it would be difficult to find... The future will probably show that for training purposes Jevington possesses very great advantages, and is possibly one of the best in the kingdom. A telegraph office has lately been opened, and increased postal facilities are likely to be granted the near future."[127]

Jevington's reputation as a training centre was greatly enhanced by the arrival of William Clay and his string of steeplechasers. Clay had had a long and successful career as a light-weight jockey and trainer, and had lived in the area since 1861.

---

[126] Illustrated Sporting and Dramatic News, March 22nd, 1902
[127] The Sportsman, December 6th, 1898

A JEVINGTON GROUP.
William Clay (left) and William Viney (Right). Arthur Clay (third right)
Racing Illustrated

The Illustrated Sporting and Dramatic News, in a profile published on January 4th, 1896, says he first came to Sussex to train for Mr Wadman in 1861, near what the paper called the small fishing village of Eastbourne. He was highly successful, clearing the board at the local races at Hastings, Eastbourne, Brighton and Lewes. When Wadman died he moved to set up as a public trainer in Jevington. He built a house and stables on Willingdon Lane, and the buildings are still there. The house is now split into several dwellings, and the main part is still called St Aubyns, after a brilliant steeplechaser Clay trained for Mr Egerton, then master of the East Sussex Foxhounds.

He was a very successful trainer through the early 1870s but then suffered the tragic loss of his two elder sons. William died in a race at Reading in 1874, and Edwin died riding in his first steeplechase. A loss from which he never recovered. Clay retired to Eastbourne in 1900, and died in 1910. He was 82 and had trained in Jevington for 40 years. The cause of death was also pneumonia and he was buried in his family grave in Jevington churchyard.

In the latter years of his life his son Arthur Clay and William Viney trained out of Clay's yard in Willingdon Lane, Jevington. Viney succumbed to an acute attack of pneumonia in 1900, aged 50 and by 1904 all training had stopped at the yard. Viney's obituaries, widely published, summarised his career as a trainer. He came to prominence in 1892 with Euclid, a chestnut three-year-old colt by Prism out of a mare by Speculum. The *Illustrated Sporting and Dramatic News* reflected on Viney's career, whose death, it said, has caused a feeling of sincere regret in Turf circles.

"Although it cannot be said that Viney was a fashionable trainer, he was a shrewd and practical one, which is not always the same thing. He had Euclid under his charge when that horse won the Lincolnshire Handicap a few years ago, and great credit was due to him for sending Euclid so fit to the post on that occasion, as the horse's legs were none of the best. A large sum of money was won over the race, although it did not appear to have the effect of making poor Viney a rich man. Jevington, where he trained for many years, is a very quiet place the nearest station being Polegate, whilst the population is mostly of an old-world or archaeological character. The adjacent Downs provide excellent galloping ground both in summer and winter. Arthur Clay, associated with the deceased for some time, intends, we believe, to carry on the business and owners who may like a quiet, secluded village for their racehorses cannot do better than communicate with him."[128]

John Hubert Moore, the 'father' of Irish steeplechasing also trained in Jevington during the 1870s. He was visited there by Horace Hayes, a visit Hayes recalls in *Among Men and Horses*, published in 1894. "At that time he was a tall, gaunt, powerful-looking man of about seventy, and a terrible 'tyrant', as they say in Ireland. When roused to anger (and faith it didn't take much to set him on), he had an effective way of clearing a room – generally after dinner in an hotel, during a race meeting or horse fair – by seizing a table, sideboard, or even a heavy chair, dashing it on the ground, and belabouring his opponents with its larger fragments. He taught his sons and stable lads to ride over the biggest country, by, as he used to boast, making them more afraid of him than of falling off. His favourite commentary on broken limbs and dislocated necks was: 'They that take by the sword, shall perish with the sword.'"

In preparation for his move, Charlie set about remodelling the house, which he called Devonshire House (now Jevington Place) in honour of the Duke of Devonshire. He also built a new yard of 40 stables. Charlie said that both the house and stables were fitted up "regardless of cost and very elaborately." The work took two years.

When *The People* visited in July 1904 it found Jevington to be a sweetly pretty hamlet. "Devonshire House, Wood's place, and the famous village church, form Jevington, which lies in a hollow between the Southdown Hills and within a practical stone's throw of Eastbourne." It was impressed with Devonshire House, which it described as an "up to date gentleman residence." The dining room was full of enormous oil paintings of Charlie in the

---

[128] Illustrated Sporting and Dramatic News, January 13th, 1900

days when he was "in the height of the swim" on some of his most famous rides, including Corrie Roy, a Cesarewitch winner; St Marguerite, who won the Guineas; Reve D'Or, who took the Guineas and Oaks; St Blaise, the Derby winner; Primrose II, a Manchester Cup winner; and the triple crown hero Galtee More.

"The New Stables - Sidar (on left), Colonel Wozac (on right)"
The Illustrated Sporting and Dramatic News
© Illustrated London News Ltd/Mary Evans

Galtee More won £22,637 [£2.8m] in prize money that season, the most successful by some margin, but his legs were not holding up well, and early the following year John Gubbins sold him to the Russian government for £20,000. Negotiations had been difficult, reportedly because of the unpredictable behaviour of the Russian representative, General Arapoff.

1898 would prove another good year for Charlie. At 43 years of age, he was still a popular choice of jockey and he kept up the regime that had allowed him to come back the year before fit and ready to race. He was still retained by Lord Rosebery and had secured Rosebery's agreement to move his horses to Jevington.

"Charlie Wood, the jockey who will ride for Lord Rosebery this year, has been hunting on the South Coast. Wood is never so happy as when on the back of a horse, and he seldom misses a day the year round without having a canter on his hack. He attributes his hardy health and good nerve to having lived a temperate life, and also to having gone to bed early. Many jockeys have ruined their constitutions through sitting up the night through at the card table and then going on to the course in the morning to ride at exercise."[129]

Wildfowler.
Winner of the St. Leger.
The joint property of Captain Freeman and Sam Darling.

---

[129] The Inquirer and Commercial News, Perth, February 25th, 1898

He also had a stroke of luck towards the end of the season when he picked up a chance ride on the Sam Darling trained Wildfowler in the St Leger. Darling loved telling the story of how Charlie got the ride.

> "Morny Cannon was engaged to ride him, but as Prince Soltykoff had a retainer on Morny Cannon, I waited until the last moment to see if he exercised his claim, which he did. I walked into the weighing-room to see if Wood was riding, and said, 'Will you ride Wildfowler for me?' Jeddah was hot favourite, and Wildfowler won by five or six lengths."[130]

Charlie collected a big fee for the win and, according to the *Illustrated Sporting and Dramatic News*, he earned more than £30,000 [£3.8m] that season, although he laid claim to a more modest £14,000.

In October 1898 the *Hull Daily Mail* reported that he was finally planning to leave Newmarket for Jevington with Rosebery's horses: "We all wish that the popular Charlie will have every success, and send out plenty of winners when he gets to his new home."

Rosebery's vote of confidence in him was significant. The former Prime Minister was a leading owner and breeder, with two Derby wins to his name at that time: Ladas in 1894 and Sir Visto in 1895. Rosebery had been desperate for Charlie to ride Sir Visto but had not been able to get his licence restored. The *Manchester Courier* commented that there could be no doubt as to the ability of his trainer, and as regards the stabling and training

---

[130] Sam Darling's Reminiscences, 1914

grounds at Jevington: "His lordship has already inspected them with complete satisfaction."[131]

By 1899 Charlie was training 24 horses in Jevington for Rosebery.

> "His has been a somewhat chequered career on the turf, but the British public invariably espouse the cause of a man whom they think has been unfortunate, and so he was warmly welcomed back when he returned to his profession two years ago.
>
> For some reason or another, too, he seemed to ride better than he had ever done at any rate he went ahead right away, and not only rode 122 winners altogether that season, but also had the good luck to be on the back of Galtee More when that good colt carried off the three classic events of the year.
>
> He has now taken up his residence at Jevington, in Sussex, where he trains for Lord Rosebery, and as that owner's Ladas youngsters are reported to be of surpassing promise, it is more than likely that Mr 'Charlie' Wood is going to have a great season."[132]

In 1899 *The Referee* went on a visit:

> "Driving among the Sussex Downs this Sunday my coachman paid homage... 'This is Jevington, sir,' he said. 'That farm yonder belongs to Mr Wood, that stretch of Downs is his private property, that is where he gallops his horses. Yonder are his stables.' A little further on we came upon a gentleman strolling down a lovely lane with his church service under his arm.

[131] Manchester Courier and Lancashire General Advertiser, December 5th, 1898
[132] Illustrated Sporting and Dramatic News, March 18th, 1899

'There he is, sir, there he is,'... The quiet gentleman turned and nodded. It was Charlie Wood, the famous jockey."[133]

In 1900 the *York Herald* reported that he won the heart of the village parson by laying on the electric light in the parish church, free of charge.[134] His winter gallop passed within yards of the church door. The summer gallops ran up the valley awards the village of Friston, known as Oxendean.

ON OXENDEAN. MESSRS J. AND C. WOOD BRINGING UP THE REAR.
TRAINING ON THE SUSSEX DOWNS. A VISIT TO JEVINGTON.

"On Oxendean. Messrs J and C Wood Bringing up the rear"
The Illustrated Sporting and Dramatic News
© Illustrated London News Ltd/Mary Evans

In 1900 Rosebery's Velasquez, the horse Charlie beat in the 1897 Derby, came to the yard and later won the Champion Stakes and Eclipse Stakes. But he failed badly as a stallion, with Rosebery later saying he had ruined half his stud.

Rosebery came regularly to view his horses and, in 1935, Charlie told the *Coventry Evening Telegraph*:

---

[133] The Referee, October 1st, 1899
[134] York Herald, February 17th, 1900

"I remember one morning Lord Rosebery was riding out with us at Jevington. We passed a sweep and I raised my hat. His lordship said, 'Why did you do that, Wood?' I replied, 'It is lucky, my lord' and Lord Rosebery immediately turned round and doffed his hat several times. Two days later I won the Eclipse Stakes for him, and ever afterwards he looked for the sweep when he came to Jevington but never saw him again".[135]

Once Charlie and his wife and daughters had settled in Jevington, his next step was to bring his son, James, home to train. To that end he set about building a yard for James at the other end of the village, on a former orchard.

James had served his training apprenticeship with Newmarket trainer Martin Gurry. He then became James Platt's head man, and later travelled with Robert Peck's horses. After his own experience as a jockey, Charlie forbade James from following him into the profession, although James seems to have been a good rider and had a brief spell as an apprentice jockey in 1898. "A promising young jockey is 'Charlie' Wood's son, who is under Platt's instructions, and will sport silk next year."[136]

By January 1899 James had moved to Jevington. Charlie's plan was to continue to ride, while establishing himself and his son as trainers. James is soon listed as training for George Faber and his first winner, Autoscope, in 1899 was ridden by his father.

1900 saw Charlie still riding in major races. He was retained by Lord Rosebery as his jockey and held a second claim from Prince Soltykoff who, as steward and arbitrator, had sat resolutely reading *Ruff's Guide* all the way through the *Chetwynd v Durham* dispute.

---

[135] Coventry Evening Telegraph, November 21st, 1935
[136] Newcastle Morning Herald, October 1898

On March 25th, 1900 'Jim the Penman' from the *Sporting Times* visited Jevington to take advantage of:

"A privileged opportunity of inspecting Lord Rosebery's horses in training… a chance not to be missed. Hence, after a long climb from Eastbourne, I found myself landed on the heights of the Jevington downs on a morning so bright and fine, in atmosphere so clear and exhilarating, that, apart from any other treat in prospect, it seemed – especially after the wretched meteorological conditions which have so long obtained – grand to be alive."

MR. C. WOOD.

The Illustrated Sporting and Dramatic News
© Illustrated London News Ltd/Mary Evans

He met Charlie, mounted on a clever-looking, clean-bred hack: "The embodiment of good health and condition." The winter had, if not particularly severe, been nevertheless a rough one for horses and men alike, the reporter said, but care and good stabling have helped to ensure a clean bill of health in the Devonshire House establishment:

"Taken for all in all, no team of horses could look brighter than that which is here sheltered. Whatever may have been the drawbacks in the way of ground condition earlier on, it would be hard to imagine anything more perfect than the going just now, the old down turf being like the proverbial Turkish carpet, and horses seemed simply to revel in their work."

Rosebery's string in Charlie's care now numbered 27 horses, including the older Tom Cringle and Flambard, nine three-year-olds, and 16 youngsters: "All of high breeding, and the majority possessed of good looks, which, deceiving as they have oftentimes proved, are still suggestive of racing merit." Oriflamb, the sire of Flambard, was standing at stud at Jevington and was well patronised. He was by Derby winner Bend Or, out of Illuminata, but was the cheapest horse at the stud, standing at the nominal fee of ten guineas, because he met with accident in his early days and never saw a racecourse.

The reporter took the opportunity to walk past the Eight Bells pub north through the village to find the newly built yard 'designed on the newest and most complete lines' where James trained. The young trainer had some horses with great bloodlines in his care.

One, Pietermaritzburg, was a colt by the stallion that had been brought to fame by Charlie, St Simon. He had been bought for 2,000 guineas and was: "A very fine colt, showing more substance than the generality of St Simon colts at that early age, and looks will not count for much should he not race [to a] merry tune." The journalist was impressed with the health of James's horses:

"To the credit of James Wood, the seventeen horses now comprising his team all look in grand trim, and, as a young trainer, he may be congratulated on the patronage of sundry owners to whom money is no object as long they can acquire horses that can win races, and with whom betting is matter of but little consideration. He has already shown his ability in the art of training, and one thing we may be sure – if the horses are good enough, so also will the man be."

"A few of the boxes at Mr J Wood's Stables"
The Illustrated Sporting and Dramatic News
© Illustrated London News Ltd/Mary Evans

The relationship with Rosebery started to weaken during 1900 as his horses were not doing consistently well. But Charlie was picking up other owners and in May 1901 *The Sketch* reported that Prince Soltykoff had sent some of his horses to him. The paper was pleased for it saw Charlie as:

"One of the smartest businessmen we have on the turf. He has had very bad luck with Lord Rosebery's horses, but in my opinion, the animals were a pretty bad lot.

Wood has a sweetly pretty house on the South Downs, and the gallops are grand, so that, with useful horses, he should win some races, and no-one would begrudge Prince Soltykoff a good win, as he is a sportsman of the first water."

In 1902 the *Illustrated Sporting and Dramatic News* took the opportunity to visit.

"A few years ago... Charles Wood, the great jockey... built new stables for himself at Jevington, improving the gallops and spared no expense to make his arrangements perfect. Starting with the horses of Lord Rosebery to train, he began well but he had a little bad luck with them, an experience which all trainers suffer now and then unless they are supernaturally endowed, which is not likely, and he failed to turn out the desired number of winners. Time was not allowed him in which to establish a decent average. When the winners were not at once forthcoming, impatience was expressed, and horses were sold...

Training since on his own account, C Wood has proved his cleverness in sending out successful flyers and he has certainly all the necessary facilities at his command. His stables are now models of their kind, being built on the latest and most approved plans, whilst the turf he has to gallop on leaves little or nothing to be desired. Of course, Wood is a thoroughly practical man in every department he knows how horses should be trained and ridden, and he can do both. His son, J Wood, also trains at Jevington, so that, locally speaking, *pere el fils* are pretty strongly in evidence."[137]

As the decade wore on, James continued to build his reputation as a trainer. *The People* visited in July 1904. "If the old adage 'like begets like' holds good, young James Wood, as the son of such a capable trainer and jockey as Charles Wood, must gain even higher honours on the turf than have been his during the short time he has presided over the unpretentious training establishment at Jevington."

There was no doubt, in the paper's view, that in time Charlie's mantle would fall upon his son: "Who in appearance is exactly a chip off the old block, and in ability apparently but little inferior." Cypka and Engineer had won for his little stable, and, "twice at Sandown the Acmena filly has given evidence of her trainer's care and ability, for he bought her very cheaply when she scrambled home in the worst class selling plate, and improved her... in six weeks. The diminutive filly won each time of competing, so although he lost her under the hammer last week, it is no wonder that Mr 'Strathern' will buy others to fill her place."

It concluded, "Jimmy Wood is a happy married man and father, does not look more than two-thirds his 28 years, never bets more than a fiver, and no one has ever known him without liking him."[138] He had married Mabel Cameron in 1901 and they had a son, Reginald James Ivor Wood in 1904.

It is clear through all the comments on both yards that Charlie and his son were horsemen who loved horses. *The People* in 1904 was impressed with Jevington as a training ground, in particular the quality of the gallops: "The surest testimony to the

---

[137] Illustrated Sporting and Dramatic News, March 22nd, 1902
[138] The People, July 24th, 1904

going is that...neither C nor J Wood have a single bad limbed horse in their boxes."

It had been a successful season for father and son. Charlie had a very useful team and James: "Has even tied the 'guv'nor' for winners this season."

> "The stable is really a little coterie — more of a happy family — glad to win for the honour's sake, rather than a betting stable making a mere machine of their horses and up to every device... [Wood] is now a grandpa, and verging on 50, but he looks 30. A real good sort. I honestly believe he is a better raconteur than a jockey. Wood has always been a home bird, and a sensible, thrifty man, not the usual style of West End jockey, so now he is dabbling more in training as a hobby, and for the occupation, not of necessity. Whether they have good horses or not, there are always good people to be met with Jevington Way."[139]

In 1905 *The Globe* said that, while trainers invariably spring from the ranks of jockeys, James Wood was the exception. "Although the son of the famous jockey and present-time trainer, Charles Wood, he has always concentrated his attention upon the treatment of the thoroughbred in the stable." When he got his own yard there was every reason to anticipate the success which so quickly followed James's individual efforts as a fully-fledged trainer: "In every way Wood may well maintain the family prestige, yet he is sensible enough to restrict the number of his team to a round dozen or so, so that every horse's peculiarities and needs can be known to him personally."[140]

[139] The People, July 3rd, 1904
[140] The Globe, January 12th, 1905

In 1906, Charlie was training for John Corlett, who in his time had written about all of Charlie's trials and triumphs for the *Sporting Times*. Corlett had three horses with Charlie, including Let Go the Painter and Detection. In 1907 Charlie was reported as having a dabble at training horses to go hurdling:

"Nearly a quarter century ago Charlie Wood was name to be respected in the Turf world, and old stagers now pronounce him as one of the finest horsemen that ever sported silk. Nowadays Wood is equally respected as a clever trainer of horses, but it is only recently that he has tampered with cross-country affairs. However, he knows how to prepare candidate to jump hurdles as well as anyone living, and did not disguise his confidence in Balavil for the Cobham Hurdle Race. Kat, who was humorously called out by the bookmakers as "pussy, pussy," was always distinct favourite, but she is an awful novice at jumping and lost so much ground at each hurdle that she could not possibly make it up the flat, and, whilst Balavil won cleverly, she was unplaced."[141]

In 1908, James moved to Doncaster to train. The reasons are not clear, but it proved a good move. The *Yorkshire Evening Post* on August 10th reported that he has been: "Wonderfully successful since he migrated from Jevington… to train for Mr Milnthorp." His first winner had been in July at Nottingham races in the Holme Pierrepont Selling Plate with Golden Prospect. By 1911 he was on the move again. "Young James Wood, the trainer, has decided to migrate to Epsom from Doncaster, and will take his team to their new quarters next Monday."[142]

---

[141] Belfast Newsletter, December 14th, 1907
[142] The Globe, February 8th, 1911

In 1911, Charlie took some horses to Ayr races:

"The once famous English jockey tells a most amusing story in regard to his visit to a shaving salon in Ayr. On the first afternoon a horse which he had very much fancied, and was one of the favourites, had been badly beaten. The next morning when getting a 'scrape', the artist would talk racing, and lamented his losses upon the horse which Wood trained, incidentally mentioning that Wood was a terrible scoundrel, and had never tried to win it. 'In fact,' he added, getting excited and quite rough with his razor, 'if I had him here I would cut his... throat.' Wood admits he got quite nervous, and, saying he felt unwell, quitted the shop half shaved."[143]

The 1911 Census showed Charlie as resident at Devonshire House with Ellen, 52, daughter Doris Victoria Violet Wood, aged 10, and granddaughter Violetta Wood, James's daughter. His staff included Thomas Grants, butler and his wife Ellen, the cook, and May Farr servant, aged 16. James was living in Epsom with his wife, Mabel and son Reginald James Ivor.

The First Word War was about to have disastrous impact on the Wood family. James was settled in Epsom and the *Newcastle Journal*, on 29th December 1916, recorded that he had received an appointment from the Army Veterinary Department.

On April 30th, 1919 the *Daily Mail* reported that during the war James had served in the remount transit department, and made many trips to the United States.

"[During] one of these his boat, the Pennsylvanian, was destroyed by a submarine and he had a narrow

---

[143] Dubbo Dispatch and Wellington Independent, June 3rd, 1911

escape with his life. The Board of Trade has awarded him the torpedo badge."

He was rescued after several hours in the water but was ill for a long time and did not reappear as a trainer until 1930. When he eventually recovered, he returned to Epsom and trained at Badminton, Tattenham Corner and Warren Farm before settling at Downs House in 1945, where he remained until his death in 1951. On his return in 1930 he was soon winning again: "Gafadoun is the first winner that James Wood, son of Charlie Wood, the jockey, has turned out since he renewed his trainer's licence."[144]

The *Bloodstock Breeders Review* said James, like his father, was always neatly dressed in dark, sober clothes (they both often sported bowler hats) and never conformed in appearance to any popular picture of a trainer or horseman.

> "Though of retiring disposition, his friends knew him as a genial and entertaining companion. His kindness was also extended to a great variety of animals for which Downs House was a sanctuary."

During his time in Jevington, Charlie embraced village life. He loved playing cricket and had been part of a team of leading jockeys, including Fred Archer, who played a team of huntsmen at Lords in 1881.

In 1909 he hosted a match between a team from Jevington and the Eastbourne Railway Porters, captained by Mr J Cordell. The Jevington team won by eight runs. Walter Stubbs, Charlie's bailiff, was one of the players and caught and bowled for no runs.[145] When the estate was later sold to Zorzis Michalinos,

---

[144] Yorkshire Evening Post, 16th August, 1930
[145] Sussex Agricultural Express, August 20th, 1909

Jevington Cricket Club, which is still active today, adopted his racing colours of pale blue and white.

Every year Charlie held a dinner for employees in the Eight Bells, a four hundred year old pub still in operation today. The dinners were often extensively reported in the local press. In 1908 the *Sussex Agricultural Express* ran the following:

"JEVINGTON. EMPLOYEES' DINNER Farm and stable hands engaged by Mr Charles Wood at his well-known racing stables at Jevington sat down on Wednesday evening their tenth annual supper, which is generously provided year by year for their enjoyment. It was served at the Eight Bells Inn by Host and Hostess F W Hemmings, who served one of the repasts identical with Sussex rural life. The company, including visitors, numbering over 40, was presided over by Mr James Wood; the vice chairs being ably filled by Mr Walter Stubbs (the popular manager of the Jevington stables) and Mr WC Carter. After doing full justice to the roast and boiled, plum puddings and mince pies, the toast of "The King" was duly honoured. Mr Walter Stubbs proposed the health of Mr Charles Wood, 'which was received with great cheering.' He remarked that Mr Wood could not be with them, but Mr James Wood was (applause). They had in Mr Charles Wood a large and liberal employer of labourers in Jevington, which was one reason such respect was paid to him and Mrs Wood (applause). Mr Carter, in a few words, said such gatherings in the country districts were a great help and prevented the spirit of Socialism, and they would not, therefore, have so much discontent and pauperism."[146]

---

[146] Sussex Agricultural Express, January 25th, 1908

As the main landlord in Jevington, Charlie's time there was not without controversy. Tied housing in estate villages was becoming a political issue in the early years of the 20th century, possibly seen by the landlords as a manifestation of the socialism mentioned at the dinner.

Matters came to a head in the village when the rector of Jevington, Edward Crake, was invited to speak at a Rural Housing Conference. He told the conference that housing conditions were so bad in his district that he knew a fourteen-year-old girl who slept in a chest of drawers in an overcrowded cottage. Four lodgers in a single room, he said, had endured those conditions without complaint until the middle of their room was occupied by a fifth lodger.

His speech was widely reported and landed Crake in hot water locally, something he said was very painful to him. It would soon become more painful. Farmer and political activist Frederick Earnest Green pulled Crake and Jevington back into the news when he published *The Tyranny of the Countryside* in 1913 – a polemic against tied agricultural housing and poor housing conditions in the countryside.

Green does not name Jevington, but he writes of a charming downland village devoid of any outward sign of poverty where: "The people were living in a state of villeinage under the rule of one or more tyrants, to whom they were beholden for their bread and butter as well as a roof over their heads."

The rector, he said, was unhappy.[147] Crake must have become even more unhappy when he later read Green's comment:

"In the same village are stables in which horses are housed in luxury, even splendour. To record the words of the good old rector, 'the horses are housed like princes and the peasants like pigs.'"

---

[147] The Tyranny of the Countryside, FE Green, 1913

The village, Green said, was ruled by two men, one represented the *nouveaux riches*, who had won his way to riches 'through keeping a safe seat on a fast horse,' in other words Charlie, and the other he calls old landed aristocracy. He was referring to Roland Gwynne, the landlord from Folkington Estate, although he was not old landed aristocracy. His father had made a fortune in the 19th century from an engineering business, and bought his estates in Sussex, centred on Folkington, the neighbouring village to Jevington, with the proceeds.

Green went drinking at the Eight Bells pub to try and get information, but: "You would not hear one word of revolt in this village symposium, carried on through the whole evening in the tap room of the inn." He then endeavoured to start conversations on the dark village street, overshadowed by elms. "No revolutionary note is sounded by these patient, docile men – not even under the stars at night."

The main dispute he uncovered was over land for allotments in the village, as Charlie had converted the existing ones into his own kitchen garden. Both landlords were refusing to release any replacement land. The housing was also clearly overcrowded in some cases, with a one bedroomed cottage housing a family of four.

Green was also concerned that, while the water in the village had to be drawn from wells, with one public well serving about 20 cottages, none of the cottages had guttering to help the tenants collect water. Close by there were waterworks, he said, "But no landlord, no public authority attempts to cleanse these Augean stables of the poor."

To Green's frustration no one was prepared to make complaints about their conditions. As one resident told him: "That's more than our place be worth – we should lose our home too."

Crake had a good record on providing housing in the village – he built three cottages for his staff and two houses for his daughters. And he may gave sought to smooth ruffled feathers when, the year the book was published, a church meeting, chaired by Crake, was recorded as passing a hearty vote of thanks to Charlie for his kindness in allowing the church to continue to use the electric light from Devonshire House, free of charge.

Charlie retired from training in 1916, the year James was called up. The war had effectively stopped racing, and he would be 62 that November.

Our Sporting Gallery: No. 12 Mr. Z. G. Michalinos
© Illustrated London News Ltd/Mary Evans

The next era of racing in Jevington started in January 1919, when Charlie sold the farm and village to Zorzis George Michalinos. Initially Michalinos did not live in Jevington, and trainer Fred Hunt lived in the house until his death in 1923.

Michalinos then decided to retire from his major shipping interests in the City of London.

> "He rebuilt a delightful house at Jevington, installed his own private trainer, F Scott, and established a breeding stud with his very smart sprinter, Pelops – one of the best bred horses in the world – as the sire. The training and breeding establishments are run on admirable lines, and Mr Michalinos will soon be showing us winners of his own breeding."[148]

Michalinos also loved his horses. In 1928, the *Sheffield Daily Telegraph* reported that trainer FB Barling, had informed their Newmarket correspondent that the horses which he had trained there for Michalinos are leaving him at their owner's request for Jevington.

> "Mr Michalinos, who lives at Jevington, misses his horses a great deal, and although they have done well since being at Newmarket, he will be glad to have them on the spot. A trainer has been engaged, but his name has not yet been divulged. Mr Michalinos won the Cambridgeshire 1919 with Zinovia, who was trained by the late F Hunt at Jevington."[149]

When Michalinos died in 1940, his nephew, Michael Tachmindji inherited the Jevington estate and after the war set up his own training and breeding yard, based around the stallion Fairey Fulmar.

In 1946 there was a match between Tachmindji's Jevington trained horse, Fairey Fulmar and James Wood's Epsom trained

---

[148] Dundee Courier, June 25th, 1926
[149] Sheffield Daily Telegraph, January 25th, 1928

Joani Star in the Cambridgeshire. Fairey Fulmar won. When the stallion died he was said to have been buried in an orchard behind the barn now known as Newton House.

The Final Years

Family Archive

After he sold his Jevington estate, Charlie spent the remainder of his days in Sussex, at Osborne House in Seaside Road, Eastbourne.

He celebrated his 81st birthday on November 21st, 1935, and he and Ellen were preparing to celebrate their diamond wedding on December 16th when the *Evening Telegraph* visited and found them both remarkably well preserved. It said they could be taken for being 20 years younger, although Charlie had suffered neuralgia a few years before and had lost his sight in his right eye, with the left also affected. Charlie told the paper he had had a wonderfully happy life, and all his children were alive and well.

With the grandchildren, they would make up a family party of about 20 for the wedding anniversary.[150] Their six children were James, Ellen, Bessie, Lizzie, Rosa and Doris. Doris was born in Jevington.

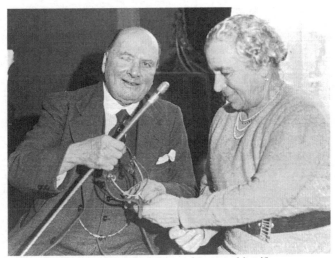

"Mr Wood showing his whip and spurs to his wife.
He used these when winning three Derbys"
Family Archive

Long retired, he was never forgotten in racing circles. The Duke of Portland, famed as one of the few honest men in racing, remained in contact well into Charlie's old age. As the *Derby Evening Telegraph* reported on December 9th, 1935:

"Although the Duke of Portland still had some horses in training, he is not the prominent figure on the turf that he was 40 or 50 years ago. His interested in racing, however, is not ended. For I see that he has just sent an autographed copy of his recently published memoirs on sporting to Charles Wood, his old time jockey. Wood, now an octogenarian, was contemporary with

---

[150] The Evening Telegraph, November 22nd, 1935

Fred Archer, and the famous Derby jockeys, Sam and Tom Loates. He rode St Simon for the Duke of Portland in all his races before that famous horse retired to stud at Welbeck. His son, James Wood, trains at Epsom. Mr and Mrs Charles Wood, who live in Eastbourne, will celebrate their diamond wedding in a few days' time."

The *London Evening Standard* published an interview with Charlie in December 1935, just after he and Ellen celebrated that anniversary, complete with a telegram from the King, under the title 'Fred Archer's Great Rival. C Wood Still Alive and Well.' Discussing his successes, Charlie said:

"The best race I rode was when I won the Derby on St. Blaise In 1883. I beat Fred Webb and Fred Archer by a neck and half a length... I was really responsible for Tod Sloan coming over. Lord William Beresford wanted me to ride first jockey for him but I had to refuse. He said: 'Well, I have got a lot of good horses, and I am not going to be disappointed over a jockey.' So he arranged for Sloan to come over. I never copied Sloan's style, although I may have shortened my leathers a couple of holes: I never thought there was much in the style. I still think the old seat as good as the new and I guarantee that if I was riding to-day I should get plenty of winners...

Then Mrs Wood had something to say, 'I never went racing, except at Newmarket, when we lived there' she admitted. 'I did once go to Ascot and see him win the Hunt Cup. 1 was happy at home with the children and was content to bank the money when he came home.' 'But she has not told you that she was a fine rider to hounds,' interposed her husband. 'She has been the best wife a man could have and we have been very happy'."

The *Evening News,* on 21st November 1936, reported on Charlie's 82 birthday under the headline Famous Ex-Jockey Thinks Betting is Foolish. He told the reporter that he was spending his birthday quietly: "I am thankful to say I am in good health… I have not been racing since I sold my place at Jevington 20 years ago, to Mr Michalinos. I think betting is a very foolish pastime. I have seen the downfall through it of so many old friends."

In 1937 John Werge thought Hull, his birthplace, would like news of their famous son.

"With the flat racing season looming on the horizon, it may interest your many racing readers to learn that Charles Wood, Hull-born jockey, celebrated his eighty-second birthday at his home at Eastbourne on November 21st last year… This famous rider was a nephew of the late Thomas Wood, the well-known butcher, whose shop in Chariot-street at the corner of Medley-street, was a well-known landmark in the days of bygone Hull. Although only a lad round about the dates named, and never interested racing, I well remember the name of Charley Wood, since his racing record at times was on almost every tongue. I am indeed surprised and pleased learn that Mr Wood is still in the land of the living."[151]

The *Calgary Herald* published a note on January 2nd 1943 when Charlie was 88. "Near his Eastbourne home small boys still

---

[151] Hull Daily Mail, February 16th, 1937

point to him as he walks down the street. They pass on to their friends the knowledge that there goes a man whose name has become a legend in British racing."

During the Second World War he had to leave his house for six months after it had been bombed and machine gunned. The *Yorkshire Evening Post* reported on September 16th 1943 that the 89 year old Charlie and Ellen had just returned to his Eastbourne house after a six month absence while it was rebuilt. They spent the six months staying with their five children and numerous grandchildren.

In 1944, Charlie celebrated his diamond wedding at his home at Eastbourne. "His five daughters and his only son, James Wood, the Epsom trainer, are all expecting to take part in the family gathering. Charlie Wood, who rode three Derby winners, and was successful in many other classic races, was 90 last month. Despite blindness, he is in good spirits. Mrs Wood enjoys perfect health."[152]

Charlie died on November 7th, 1945 aged 90, just before his 91st birthday, leaving £60,000 in his will. The *Times* marked his passing.

"Charles Wood, whose death took place at Eastbourne on Saturday at the age of 90, was the last of that famous band of jockeys who, with great horses and great trainers, made the 80s and 90s of the last century the Augustan age of horse-racing. Wood rode against men like Fordham, Archer, Tom Cannon, Goater, Custance, Constable, Webb, Watt, Maidment and John Osbourne and during his career won 1,750 races.

He won the Derby three times, on St Blaise, St Gatien (dead heat) and Galtee More, The St Leger on Galtee More and Wildfowler, and was successful in all the

---

[152] Coventry Evening Telegraph, December 15th, 1944

other classic races. He [rode the] great St Simon and seven times he was second to Archer in the list of winning jockeys before he headed the list himself in 1887. His career was interrupted for a time as the result of the famous *Chetwynd – Durham* libel action, but he was not the man to go to seed during enforced retirement and he was successful as ever on his return to the saddle when his first mount [sic] was given him by Lord Durham, whose speech at a Gimcrack Club dinner had caused all the trouble.

Wood trained for a time after he had finished riding and also helped his son James, who now has a successful stable at Epsom. He had never had the trouble with his weight that brought ill health to many of his famous contemporaries, and until he was nearly 80 had the best of health. Seven years ago he lost the sight of an eye and latterly he was almost completely blind. He remained however, remarkably active in his mind, and last year celebrated with his wife the sixty-ninth anniversary of their wedding. It is nice to record that they had a bottle of champagne with their lunch."

Ellen Wood died on 27th August 1949.

POSTSCRIPT

Charles Wood

Redemption and Vindication

Now that it is all over I will tell you on my word of honour I was wrongly punished – I never pulled Success

Charlie rose to fame and wealth at the same time as Fred Archer. They were very similar – ambitious, skilful horsemen who used their abilities to become wealthy in their own right. Both were highly successful as jockeys and businessmen. Both suffered constant attacks for dishonesty and corruption.

The rumours of large bets surrounding Fred Archer are more talked about in the records of the time and they appeared in various print forms over his short career. His tragic and untimely death extinguished one of the greatest jockeys of all time and he is still rightly revered for his skill as a jockey.

The tragedy for Charlie was that, if he had not been banished for nine years, his record might well have stood shoulder to shoulder with Archer. On Derby winners alone, Charlie had three against Fred's five. During his exile, Lord Rosebery made it clear that he wanted Charlie to ride St Visto in the 1895 Derby. St Visto won with a different jockey. The year before Rosebery's Ladas also won the Derby.

It was after Fred Archer committed suicide at the end of 1886 and Charlie rose to become champion jockey that the full force of the Jockey Club's retribution for daring to fly so high descended on his head. Rumours of roguery were rife, as ever, in racing and the Jockey Club, and in particular Lord Durham, decided someone had to be sacrificed.

The lamb chosen for slaughter was Charlie. He was the most successful jockey after Archer and, as the Jockey Club members almost certainly knew he was born out of wedlock, they were faced with the possibility of a bastard leading the championship for many years to come. To add insult to injury, many of its members were increasingly angry at the way some jockeys and trainers were becoming independent and wealthy in their own right, free of the controlling hand of their would-be masters. In their determination to reassert their authority, Charlie must have looked an easy target. A champion jockey, with many powerful friends, would normally be seen as difficult to attack; unless the target was an illegitimate runaway from the slums of Hull, with no rights and no breeding.

The sense of injustice Charlie must have felt would have been exacerbated by the knowledge that none of the specific allegations brought to court were proved against either himself, Richard Sherrard or Sir George Chetwynd. Chetwynd had resigned from the Jockey Club, but many thought, including himself, that his offer to resign had been too hasty. Sherrard was banished from Newmarket but allowed to train elsewhere. Charlie was banned from riding, owning or training racehorses. He could not even attend a race. It was an unprecedented seven years before he was allowed back onto the Heath and nine before he was allowed to ride in races again.

Once they had decided on their target the Jockey Club and their lawyers threw every vague allegation and rumour they could dig up at Charlie. They employed private detectives to find evidence of pulling horses and found nothing. The best they could manage was a stable lad who said he knew when Charlie was pulling a horse by the way he sat (to the amusement of the spectators in court), who was not believed by the jury, and a jockey who claimed he had been told to pull Chetwynd's Fullerton, who was not believed by the arbitrators. The most they managed to get was an admission that he had an interest in one, or maybe more, horses, in breach of the rule barring jockeys from owning horses. But, as racing commentators at the time said, the complex multiple ownership of horses, including by jockeys, was widespread across the industry.

After the trials Sir Francis Lawley condemned the first trial's judge, Lord Coleridge, and the Jockey Club stewards sitting as arbitrators in the second trial, for allowing the admission of evidence on reputation based on idle rumours. Lawley saw Charlie as a victim from the moment Durham targeted him in his speech at the Gimcrack Dinner.

> "The reputation of a successful jockey was sneered away without any specific crime or malpractice being laid to his charge, or, as has since been proved, without Lord Durham being able to substantiate his words. It was as impossible for Wood to fight Lord Durham's 'glittering generalities' as for him to destroy at one blow a swarm of mosquitoes buzzing around his ears... None are so incorrectly judged by their fellows as those who have quickly made money and acquired fame. 'A city set upon a hill cannot be hid.'"

Charlie's appeal against the order for costs in his case showed in no uncertain terms that even the judiciary was content to condemn him on his perceived reputation alone. The Master of the Rolls, Lord Esher, made the extraordinary statement that, while the jury was conclusive that Charlie did not pull Success: "A man with such a character as Wood had no right to bring the action, and acted oppressively in doing so, and therefore good cause existed for depriving him of costs." A decision that also ignored the fact that the Jockey Club had made it plain he would not get his licence unless he brought the action.

After the two libel trials, some commentators condemned Charlie and Chetwynd for dragging racing into a public scandal, again conveniently ignoring the fact that both had been required by the Jockey Club to sue to attempt to clear their names.

His training record in Jevington, when he had direct care of his horses, showed that he was a true horseman. His horses were kept to a very high standard. They were not over trained and in the main were injury free. When he was a jockey, Mathew Dawson said he did not abuse his horses, and as a trainer the same was true. That love of horses is one of the keys to his success, but the Jockey Club took no regard of the man and his qualities, they just wanted him cut out of racing.

If the Jockey Club was influenced by the fact that he was illegitimate or Jewish, it was never publicly stated, but the severity of his treatment was more extreme than any of his contemporary jockeys at that time.

Charlie left no one in any doubt that he had neither forgotten nor forgiven; and that to win the Derby in 1897 in front of his main persecutors was a sweet moment. When the *Pall Mall Gazette* cornered him after the race the article, published on June 5th, 1897, underlined why he was still the best jockey in the country – a skilled and intelligent horseman who rode his race with good judgement. He knew the capabilities of his own mount and the capabilities of the other jockeys and horses in the race.

> "[Galtee More] came down the hill as nicely as he could possibly do and at the turn into the straight I had a good look round to see where the danger was to come from. I knew even then the Prince's horse was nearly out, and so was History, and the only fear I had to face was Velasquez. His exact measure I took in the

straight, where I could see Jack Watts getting uneasy on Lord Rosebery's horse. It was truly an easy ride for me, as I had only to sit where I was to be the first to see Judge Robinson."

He finished the interview with a clear statement:

"Now that it is all over I will tell you on my word of honour I was wrongly punished – I never pulled Success."

Sir George Chetwynd in his memoir, *Racing Reminiscences and Experiences of the Turf,* written in 1891, while Charlie was still banished, was in no doubt that the way the Jockey Club set about seeking to destroy Charlie and completely banish him from racing was unprecedented and wrong.

"I ask my readers, what really serious offence was ever proved against Wood throughout two long trials? Certainly not that he had ever pulled a horse. All that came out against him was what he confessed himself, viz., that he had broken the rules of the Jockey Club by owning horses when he was forbidden to do so...
No doubt he committed an offence in owning horses when he was expressly told he was not to do so; but what has been his punishment? After it had cost him thousands of pounds to prove that he did not pull Success – and every man who knows anything about racing now fully understands the baselessness of the charge – his licence has been taken away, and he has been virtually warned off the Turf as if he were an ordinary welsher or thief.

The written law of England defines a period of punishment for every offence; the unwritten law of the Jockey Club gives life sentences as it chooses!"

When Chetwynd wrote that in 1891, Charlie had been banished since 1888. That already seemed a harsh sentence. How he felt after Charlie was banned until 1897, enduring nine long years of exile, is not recorded.

Galtee More and Charlie Wood
Mary Evans Picture Library

"One finds no satisfactory reason why Wrights should
be "Shiner" and Taylors "Buck"; but it is easy to see
why a man named Wood is called "Charlie". This is a
tribute to Charlie Wood, a jockey very popular last
century, not only for his personality but for his way of
riding a spectacular finish."[153]

---

[153] Popular nicknames have queer origins By Vaughan Dryden, Gloucester Citizen
December 1944

With thanks

To Tim Cox for giving me access to his extensive racing library, The Cox Library, and starting me on this journey - www.thecoxlibrary.com

To Ian Wood and Sue Staines, Charles Wood's great grandchildren, for their help and encouragement.

To Fizz Carr and Steve Goldman for their editing.

To Jo-Anne Richards from All About Writing for her suggestions and edits on the final draft.

Sources of Illustrations, with thanks

The Mary Evans Picture Library: www.maryevans.com

The British Library Board - The British Newspaper Archive
    www.britishnewspaperarchive.co.uk

Racing Illustrated

Sam Darling's Reminiscences

Duke of Portland, Memories of Racing and Hunting

Vanity Fair

The Wood Family

The Badminton Library: Racing and Steeplechasing

Alamy Ltd

Online resources

British Newspaper Archive

Trove - National Library of Australia

Papers Past - National Library of New Zealand

Welsh Newspapers Online

Newspapers+ by Ancestry

The Bank of England Inflation Calculator

Bibliography

Astley, Sir John, Fifty Years of My Life, 1894

The Duke of Beaufort, assisted by Alfred ET Watson,
  – The Badminton Library: Racing and Steeplechasing, 1886

Black, Robert, Jockey Club and its Founders, 1891

Booth, JB, Old Pink 'un Days, 1924

Booth, JB, Old Pink 'un Remembers, 1937

Burton, James Glass, A Mirror of the Turf, 1890

Chetwynd, Sir George, Racing Reminiscences and
  – Experiences of the Turf, volumes 1 and 2, 1891

Cook, Theodore Andrea, A History Of The English Turf, 1901

Darling, Sam, Sam Darling's Reminiscences, 1914

Day, William, Turf Celebrities I have known, 1891

Day, William, William Day's Reminiscences Of The Turf, 1886

Forster, CA, Court Housing in Kingston Upon Hull, 1972

Gould, Nat, Sporting Sketches, 1900

Green, FE, The Tyranny of the Countryside, 1913

Hayes, Horace, Among Men and Horses, 1894

Humphris, Edith M, The Life of Fred Archer, 1934

Humphris, Edith M, The Life of Mathew Dawson, 1928

Lambton, Hon George, Men and Horses I have Known, 1924

Lawley, Francis, The Bench and the Jockey Club, 1889

Nevill, Ralph, The Gay Victorians, 1930

Onslow, Richard, The Squire, 1980

Pinfold, John, Horse Racing and the Upper Classes in the
  19th Century – Sport in History, 2008

Plumptree, George, The Fast Set, 1985

Duke of Portland, Memories of Racing and Hunting, 1935

Duke of Portland, Men, Women, and Things:
  – Memories of the Duke of Portland, 1937

Radcliffe, John, Ashgill: The life and times of John Osborne, 1900

Richardson, Charles, The English Turf, 1901

Scott, Alexander, Turf Memories Of Sixty Years, 1924

Thormanby (William Dixon), Kings of the Turf, 1898

Watson, Alfred E. T., The Racing World And Its Inhabitants, 1904

Welcome, John, The Life and Times of Fred Archer, 1967

Witt, John George, The Three Villages, 1904

Charlie's great grandchildren, twins Ian Wood and Sue Staines,
at Charlie and Ellens' grave, Ocklynge Cemetery, Eastbourne 2018